Everybody Kneeling

ain't praying

Everybody Kneeling

ain't praying

~A Memoir

Tara Tucker

TUCKER
PUBLISHING HOUSE LLC

Other Books
by Tara Tucker

Going Higher 12 weeks of reflection for the woman of God

Screams from the Church Pew (Anthology)

Table of Contents

DEDICATION

∿

Lord, I thank you. You've come into my life and given me a new one. Your mercy, love, and grace are unparalleled. Where would I be without You? As Nicodemus asked, "How is it possible for an adult to be born?" John 3:4a (CEB) You've shown me how possible it is. Thank you for a new life.

I also dedicate this book to my mother. You wanted to write a book, and I hope this gives you honor. There is more to come, Mommy. I think of you daily. I miss you more than mere words could describe. You are my writing inspiration. You were a diamond in the rough, the rose that grew from the concrete. You always believed in me, even when I didn't. Love you always. R.I.P.

And to Daddy: I miss you, Daddy. I miss your smile and your laugh. I miss our talks. Change is possible, and I love the progression of our relationship. I will miss you forever. I love you always.

Rest in peace to my grandmother, Lucille Poe. I love and miss you.

"Has the Lord redeemed you?
Then, speak out! Tell others He
has redeemed you from your
enemies."

—Psalms 107:2 (NLT)

FOREWORD

My name is Rita Fields, and I am Tara's friend. We attend the same church. I have known her for several years, and I have often been drawn to her spirit, without knowing why. I have always felt as though we were kindred sisters who had both been through a lot and had lived to tell it. I always sensed in her an unapologetic honesty that has also marked my existence but is sometimes rare in others. After reading this manuscript, I now understand why. I consider it a tremendous honor that she asked me to write the foreword and pray that I honor her effort and God's work in her via this small contribution.

This book is truth. It is a deliberate revealing of Tara's heart and mind and even her body in so many ways. One of the most undervalued elements of Christianity is our God-given obligation to share our testimony. I believe that God's testimonies are His, and we are merely chosen to carry them. Consequently, I don't believe we are authorized to edit them for 'more palatable consumption.' It is a rare individual who is truly so comfortable with herself and God's miraculous presence in her life that she can open her proverbial cloak and expose herself in this way. I'm so grateful that she did, as it affords me yet another view of God's consistent majesty in the lives of His children. We all have stories, but as Tara expresses in this labor of love, many of us are hiding them and living in shame. As a sister who has also experienced difficult moments in her life, I have learned that healing is available to me as I am vulnerable in sharing my struggles. We are our brothers' (and sisters') keepers, and often the ability of an individual to completely bare themselves for the possibility that it may save another the same pain is what differentiates many who identify themselves as Christians from those who endeavor to truly walk with Christ.

I am writing this foreword to wholeheartedly endorse and support Tara's commitment to sharing her story, despite the pain and discomfort it may have caused her in the recollection and the telling of said story. I believe that this book will release people from the chains that the enemy has wrapped around many lives and that it will be a conduit to the deliverance and peace that God desires for each of us. I pray that you receive this testimony as an additional reason to praise our Lord for his providence and deliverance in a world that is too often self-centered and dismissive of others' pain. I pray that you are released yourself from the pain you carry.

Thank you, Tara, for walking in your destiny. God bless your words and His plan for those who read them.

Sincerely,

Dr. Rita Fields

INTRODUCTION

I've sat in hotel rooms, apartments, and offices in commercial buildings, selling myself; Literally. I convinced myself that because I was not walking the street, I was upscale. We do that as people. We make comparisons. "I make more money than you, so the debauchery I engage in is acceptable. You, of course, are low class and just nasty." Oh, the lies we tell ourselves.

For the bulk of my life, I thought I was in control. I made great money and took care of myself. I did what I wanted, loved who I wanted, and had sex with whomever I wanted. There were little to no rules in my life. I thought I was living my best life. My thinking was jaded because of all that I saw from childhood until an adult.

Who is faithful? People are liars, and everyone played games. My world revolved around men, women, money, drinking, and weed. In a nutshell, sex was a driving factor for me. It gave me power over my prey. I didn't realize I was a predator until later in life after many sessions with my therapist, Dr. Matthews. I had some serious issues. But they weren't my fault.

Children are vulnerable. They are sponges soaking in words spoken to them and the environment in which they are planted. They thrive or wither away based on the conditions. Just as a natural plant needs good soil, sunlight, and water, children need love and protection.

My mom loved me the best way she knew how. I know that now, as a mother myself. My dad, sister, and brother tolerated me.

I didn't resemble anyone in my family, so *where the heck did I come*

INTRODUCTION

from? That was the daily question asked in my head.

"You're adopted," my sister would say, and I would cry.

"Am I adopted?" I would ask my mom.

"No, you came out of me," she would reply and sternly look and speak to my sister about such talk.

She eventually admitted that my daddy—the only daddy I've ever known—was not my biological father. He was only the biological dad to my brother and sister. That explains it, I thought. I wasn't his, and he didn't want me. But I'm the middle child. This family dynamic was confusing.

From a child onward, I looked for acceptance first in my household and then from whomever would show me attention. I would adjust myself to be who they wanted. So, my acting career—for lack of a better word—began early.

As I matured in age, I had no clue who I was and was often angry. My body became a commodity, and I learned how to use it for my benefit. Being rejected even while in the womb (I'll tell you about it later) and throughout my life put me on a destructive path, and only God could save me.

Sexually, I was fluid and did not think choosing was necessary. Live and let live was my motto.

I used to look in the mirror and see staring back at me as a temptress. I would adorn myself with colored contacts, lashes, fake hair, and full-face makeup daily to create a new persona, one that people desired. My clothes were always few as possible because I had a nice figure, and my thinking was if you had it flaunt it. I would get attention everywhere I went, but for the wrong reasons. The world was a stage, and I was an award-winning actress. Ha!

Children nor marriage were in my plans for my life. I just wanted to make money and have fun on my terms.

Cancer certainly wasn't in my plans; neither was losing both parents, cousins, and countless friends. Being saved and going to church either; I certainly metamorphosed into a new creature.

My life was full of twists and turns. I went from a debased mind to a renewed one, full of the Holy Ghost and ministering to people.

How did I get here?

This book spans three years, so keep that in mind when you're reading. Writing this book took me on an emotional rollercoaster, addressing situations I wanted to forget.

Then my dad died in October of 2017, and I stopped writing altogether. The Lord continually told me to complete it, and so in 2018, I started writing again, trusting God and walking by faith and not sight.

In this book, I am writing about an identity journey—not every detail of my entire life.

Furthermore, I have received prophetic words regarding my testimony and how it would help many. However, it wasn't until I was diagnosed with stage 3 breast cancer that I received a specific word from the Lord that there is a book inside me waiting to be

INTRODUCTION

written, and it was time to write the book of my testimony.

After initial hesitation, I warmed up to the idea because people are hurting and thinking they are unworthy of God's love or anyone's. I want them to know that God loved us first before we even knew who He was. In fact, He called me out of my mess. I wasn't looking to be saved.

This is for you: the liar; the homosexual; the one with the religious spirit; the double-mind; the prostitute; the fornicator; the angry one; the fighter; the smoker; the drunk—yes, this book is for you. The one who repeatedly messes up; the one who feels unworthy. Also, for the one who doesn't know how to love himself/herself; The one who thinks they don't measure up; the one who compares themselves to others. I was all those things. But God will use your failures for His glory! Hold your head up!

From my story, you will see how one touch in 2010 was all I needed to propel me on my journey to finding out my true identity. This was therapeutic for me—a sort of purging. We live and go through trials, pushing on; many times, we don't have to confront the past or relive anything. I had to face and relive my past through this writing.

I see how far I've come in my walk with the Lord and how lost I was in the world. I was blinded from the truth. I had a way in my eyes that was the right way to live as it says in the scriptures at Proverbs 21:2 (KJV), "Every way of man is right in his own eyes, but the Lord pondered the hearts."

How many have experienced what I have, I wonder? How many are still in mental bondage from their past? I was in captivity

INTRODUCTION

for years, and if I don't walk circumspectly even today, I will be again. The enemy tries me regularly in one way or another to imprison my thoughts again.

I've learned not to despise my trials, as they've taught me patience, endurance, and how strong I am.

In my memoir, I have changed some people's names to protect their identity; I am not trying to embarrass anyone or hurt them. It isn't even about them. This is my story, my life, and my experiences.

God has gone before me; He qualified and positioned me for greatness despite my faults, trials, and failures.

Even though I speak candidly, it's important to realize I am not glorifying the life I led. I want you to hear me in these pages and see how God worked *through* and *in* my life.

This is not a Christian book, per se; it's a memoir written by a woman who now lives for and follows Jesus Christ.

My prayer is that this book will help the lost and emotionally crippled, the one with the wall up, the one who doesn't like to be alone and jumps from relationship to relationship, and those suffering from various forms of abuse.

God is a Deliverer! He is a Healer! He is a Keeper! He is a Waymaker!

He has been that to me and so much more. He can also be those things to you if you allow Him. Come on this journey with me as I

INTRODUCTION

openly speak about my past and lead you to the present, where I am excited about my future.

Change is possible. Don't let anyone hold you hostage, because of your past. There is freedom in Jesus Christ.

Everyone has a story. This is mine. Open and Authentic.

Tara Tucker

RUSSIAN ROULETTE

Wikipedia describes Russian roulette as "a lethal game of chance in which a player places a single round in a revolver, spins the cylinder, places the muzzle against their head, and pulls the trigger."

This is what I was doing with my life, playing Russian roulette. Each stranger I opened the door to and let in could have killed me. That is a scary reality but didn't scare me enough to quit. As with any dangerous venture, we think, "It won't happen to me." The money was great, yet the danger was real. I remember one guy who scared me a bit, and I had to handle him carefully. He was new to me, but he had great reviews from previous Providers (other Escorts) because I checked. He came to me, seemingly nice. Our phone conversations were brief, but no warning lights went off inside me.

He called from the parking lot, alerting me to his presence. I then gave him the room number and instructions on how to find my room. I checked the mirror. Long, wavy blonde hair hanging to my lower back, hazel-brown eyes, pink pouty lips, and a beautiful Blasian (Black +Asian) face staring back at me. I was not Asian, but my makeup enhanced my almond eyes, and I had a biracial girl's appearance. It paid to advertise yourself as biracial in this business.

I turned around to check my backside. My black teddy was full of lace. I was slender then with big breasts, a small waist, and a supple bottom. Well-proportioned, not like the new craze of today of false bottoms not well proportioned. I slipped on my studded stilettos, a request made by Jeff, my client who was on his way up to see me.

Knock, knock, knock. I quickly ran to the door and peeked through the peephole. I saw a tall white man with brown hair and a little stubble on the chin standing outside my door. I opened the door as I stood behind it. I didn't want to take the chance of someone seeing me in my undress as they walked by.

He walked in, and I hugged him. "Hi, Jeff. So nice to meet you."

He smelled good. He held me and whispered in my ear, "Hey, Megan. You look even better in person." His voice was deep and husky.

I smiled, and I released him. "Come in and get comfortable." I walked over to the wine. "Would you like a glass of wine and some fruit?"

"Sure. Just wine." He said as he sat on the couch. "Nice room."

"Thanks," I said, smiling and pouring us some wine. I had booked a suite for the weekend in Pittsburgh. I often traveled in my profession.

"I hate when girls get dumps."

I laughed. "Yeah, I know. Well, you attract who you are." I sat down next to him as I handed him his glass.

We laughed and talked a bit. Jeff scheduled an hour and a half session, so that was $550. My eyes quickly scanned the room to see where he placed the money. I noticed the money on the bedside table. Six one-hundred-dollar bills spread out so I could see the tip he was leaving me. *Nice*, I thought.

He immediately started rubbing my leg. *Okay, so he wants to get right to it*, I thought. You never knew how these sessions would go. Every man was different. Sometimes I got paid just to converse; other times, it was a paid dinner date. Yet still another time would be tying him up and whipping him. Contrary to popular belief, it's not always sex.

I motioned to the bed and said, "Let's get comfortable over there."

I had already drunk a bottle of wine, and it was only 11:30 AM. Jeff was my third client of the day. I scheduled myself to work from 8 AM to 8 PM. I had five more clients coming, and without drinking, I wouldn't be able to make it through.

What happened next caught me off guard. Jeff got up, picked me up, and threw me on the bed. He was into rough sex; I would soon find out. He undressed and put his condom on. I was still in character, nervously laughing, trying to calm myself, and slowing him down. But to no avail. He made sure we used up his entire time, and I wondered how I would make it the rest of the day.

That $50 tip wasn't even worth it. Jeff was rough, almost to the point of violence. It seemed he got off on making me squirm, and not in a good way. I was to the point of tears. "That was great. I'm going to book you again when you come back in town," he said, smiling as he left the room. *No chance,* I thought. *Never gonna happen.*

I slowly got up and put the chain on the hotel door, called my next client to cancel. I needed some time to recover. I made a bath and soaked, got my mind right, drank some more, and lit a blunt.

This was my life now. I was an escort, a high-class prostitute. I hated the word prostitute. In my mind, an escort was different. It's the lie I told myself to cope with what I was doing for a living.

I did it to take care of my daughter. Tyler was only a few years old, and I was a single mother because her dad and I broke up. The money was a strong magnet. You see, I only had to work a few days a week to get money that people made in a month.

Sometimes, while working these hotels, I would get paranoid— especially out of town. Did the front desk suspect? I would go there, looking as normal and downplayed as possible. It was important after checking in to use side doors and not being in people's faces often. We got our extra towels and whatever we needed from them upfront, hung the "Do Not Disturb" sign on the door, and kept it moving.

My girl and I traveled together, and we loved to shop after work or on our last day before we drove or flew out. Sometimes at the end of the night, we would go to one another's room, have a drink, discuss the clients, laugh at the funny ones, and warn each other about others.

Nothing was weird or wrong for me because of the people I was around and the world I created for myself—a world where I was in control. I called the shots and being in control was important to me. I hated feeling vulnerable or like I needed anyone.

This life became normal. I would go out of town so much and throw my mom hundreds of dollars to keep an eye on my daughter Tyler. When she was older, Tyler confided in me that we didn't have as close of a relationship as her baby sister, and I had.

She said, "Mommy, you were with Devin more than you were with me. I was with Grandma."

And she was right. I bought Tyler whatever she wanted and needed, but she didn't have my time. The strangers in the hotel rooms had it.

Each john I slept with chipped more of "me" away. Every time it was like I was dying a little, losing me, my soul, mind, and emotions. Who was I? I lied to every man to stay in character. I just didn't know anymore. Living this life blurred the lines. *Was there even a line?* I was going with the flow, but where was this current leading me?

FAMILY DYNAMICS

I shouldn't be here. If my biological father had been successful in his attempts when he stabbed my pregnant mother, there would be no me. You remember the cult in Waco, Texas, headed by David Koresh, which shocked the country? Yeah, well, this isn't as tragic, but it bears mentioning.

On E. Grand Blvd, in Detroit, Michigan, in the mid-'70s, my mom met and fell in love with a hippie who was to become my biological father. I've never seen nor met this man, but I bear his features from my uncle's descriptions.

As the story goes, she told me that she and my daddy had split up in Mississippi, and she came to Detroit. My stepdad was the only dad I knew, so I refer to him as "Daddy" and the other as my biological father.

My mom, daddy, and my sister Jade were born in Mississippi. My brother Len and I were born in Detroit, Michigan.

My mom came to Detroit, and Daddy stayed behind in Mississippi because, as she told it to me, "we separated." Later I found out why.

She met my biological father in Detroit and was swept off her feet with his freckles, long hair, and short cocky stature. "He had light skin, laughing eyes, and was a good time." She explained that it was a "whirlwind romance."

Okay, so let me tell you something equally interesting and disturbing about my biological father. My mom revealed as I got older and continued to be persistent in questioning her. She wanted me to leave it alone, but I wouldn't.

My mom met my biological father at age 21/22. She thought he was "very handsome and nice." She said he lived off E. Grand Blvd on the east side of Detroit not too far from Motown studios, in one of those large, beautiful homes. This was in 1975. She said a group of people were all living there and were very spiritual, and she loved how they loved each other and had a community.

She said there was one man who was the leader, whom everyone looked up to and followed. I can't recall this man's name, but my mom said they all would eat together, and the leader would speak, and everyone listened. They prayed together, and so forth. She loved it!

Now, this is when the story took a turn. Once the group was gathered in one place, praying on their knees, something made my mom open her eyes and lookup. At this time, she was pregnant in her final trimester with me, and my sister was five years old.

She looked up and saw black shadow figures over everyone's head.

I was like, "Momma, are you serious?"

And she said, "Yes, very serious."

So, that night, she told my biological father about it and said that she wanted them to leave.

My biological father told the leader, and the leader told him to kill my mom. It sounds like a movie. Whew! I know now that Satan was trying to take me out before I even got here! So, that same night, my biological father came into the room, and they began fighting.

He stabbed my mom in the stomach. My sister was hiding under the bed while he stooped down, flinging the knife back and forth, stabbing her in the arm. She still has the scar. He also stabbed his brother and brother's wife, and my mom said he left out the window through the fire escape.

Somebody called the police and ambulance, and my biological dad was on the run. My mom said they never caught him.

She was immediately rushed to the hospital, blood everywhere. They didn't think I would make it. I was born that night, November 4, 1976.

Now, this is absolutely crazy. *Who does that?* I thought it sounded like a Lifetime movie.

While in the womb, my biological father rejected me. That's how I looked at it. And whose DNA do I carry? I would often think, what kind of man is he today? Conceived in love, but there was a tragedy surrounding my birth. It was by the grace of God that I'm here today.

One of my uncles later told me that he wanted to kill my biological father for what he did to my mom and sister but couldn't find him. I never understood how he disappeared.

Where did he go?

Shortly after, my mom went to Mississippi and reunited with her husband, my daddy. He had two other children as well, in Mississippi—a son and daughter.

As I grew, I became increasingly aware that I looked different and was treated differently than my siblings. My mom was my tower; she is where I would find safety. She was everything to me, and we were very close. As I got older, I asked who my biological father was after she admitted that the one, I thought was my biological father wasn't. She wouldn't even tell me his name. My uncles told me his "cult" name was Abulabu, and then my mom said his name was Billy Smith.

That didn't sound honest from this honest woman. But it could have been his name. I don't know because I didn't know any Black people with that name, but she said his mother was white, so I thought it possible to be named Billy Smith. Look, I was from the projects and didn't know any "Billy Smiths."

I tried to find him when I was in my early 20s but didn't have much to go on in the way of information. She didn't want me looking for him because of the hurt that he'd caused her.

I understood, but this was about *me;* the innocent "didn't ask to be born" child, not about their relationship.

She would refer to Daddy every time I inquired about my biological father and say, "He is your daddy."

Yes, I understood that, but I promise you Daddy was never a "daddy" to *me* until I became an adult, and I didn't feel as if I belonged. I desperately wanted to know where I came from and who I was.

My mom didn't understand how I truly felt. This conversation was uncomfortable for her, and she would avoid it. My mom knew her biological dad. She looked like her siblings and like her dad. I was curious to see someone else who looked like me, and I wanted a daddy who would love me.

When she told me the story, I looked surprisingly at her. It sounded like a movie script. "So, my daddy didn't want me?" I asked her, sadly.

"He was under the influence of control. I don't know if they were using drugs or what. But he wasn't in his right mind when it came down to the leader." My mom responded.

It didn't make me feel better because I saw a father who tried to kill me. I learned early that neither my daddy or biological loved or wanted me.

After that craziness, she and Daddy got back together, and my brother was born four years later. I'm in the middle of my daddy's two biological children. People would come to question this because I am in the middle, different in both looks and character than my siblings, who resemble Daddy in both.

Even though my biological father did those terrible things, I felt like so much time had passed, and he might have changed. Maybe he was sorry and wanted me? He was under the cult's influence—and probably drugs too. But I would never get an opportunity to find out. I can't say that it was easy growing up, not knowing who my biological father was. It wasn't. It was something that never left me.

Even now, I wonder if my biological father is still alive? Do I have other siblings? Grandparents, Aunts, and Uncles? Like, I think of this stuff, and I am over 40 years old. The curiosity doesn't go away. I even searched Facebook recently, to no avail. A girl needs her dad to love her first before she meets the boys. Her dad should show her the way they should treat her. Her dad should tell her she's pretty, so she's not looking for the boys' validation. Being that I didn't have that I needed and sought after it.

Recently a friend was sharing her childhood story with me. She got to the part of her dad picking her up and kissing her on the cheek. She said he would often do that. She was a self-professed "Daddy's girl" ... I had no clue what it was like to be a "Daddy's girl." I listened intently to her story, asking her what it was like to have a dad like that. She said, "It was everything. My dad was everything to me."

Wow.

Now that was something!

My childhood wasn't all terrible. I buried the bad deep inside and chose to focus on the good. I did this when bad things happened to me. In my home, almost daily, there was music playing, singing, and dancing.

I knew how to sing the blues before I heard any R&B or rap music. Gospel music was "of the devil" and certainly not played in my home as a child or even in my house as an adult until I met Jesus. But I digress.

Mom and dad loved to dance; in fact, if anyone were to speak of them, they would mention their dancing. I still love to dance today because of them. Music is a big part of my life because of Momma and Daddy. I choose to remember those musical moments because there was happiness, love, and laughter amidst the mess.

FAMILY DYNAMICS

SIBLINGS

My earliest memory in my childhood home on E. Willis was at eight years old. I noticed that I didn't look like anyone that was around me. Everyone had brown skin, and mine was light; I had freckles and moles and didn't see my face on anyone. My sister and brother had brown skin and looked like mom and dad, so I believed my sister when she said Momma adopted me. However, my mom assured me that I was all hers and came from inside of her. That solved one mystery, but not the "Why does my sister hate me?" mystery.

As children, my sister treated me as if I shouldn't be there in the home. This treatment continued as we grew older. It was weird. I loved her so much and looked up to her, but I continuously felt rejected by her. The only person who loved me was my momma.

Over the years, my sister and I tried talking about our issues at various times. My mom even intervened sometimes. But to no avail.

Daddy would say to us in a stern voice, "Stop with all that foolishness!" without looking up from the scratch-off ticket that had his attention. He would scratch, win, or lose, and grab another, continuously scratching until he'd used them all.

He was not a talker about anything serious and would defer us to mom. My sister and I don't agree on what the genuine issues were, of course. We each have our perspectives, so we left it alone, and moved on without addressing it.

Dysfunction became comfortable.

Jade and I have never had that sisterly bond. I have never experienced a close relationship with my siblings. Yet, it's beautiful when I see it in others.

Jade had a considerable influence on me as a child, and it continued into adulthood. Even though I looked up to her, as I said before, I felt like she didn't like me. We had some run-ins for real. Like the time when I stayed upstairs from her in a family flat on Baldwin off Mack, and we argued. I told her to stop overstuffing my washing machine, and if she couldn't or wouldn't, she had to stop using it. I went down to wash my clothes and found that the cord to my washer and dryer were both cut. That was her reply.

It was time for me to move out.

Then there were times where she would give me a birthday card that was so beautiful. She always picked out the best cards. Seriously. And I would say, "Who is *this,* Jade?" I didn't recognize her; Jade has a genuinely kind side to her.

There were rare moments where she was there for me, and I cried to her about something I was going through. We did have 'sister' moments if I can call it that. It wasn't all bad, especially when I was drinking and hanging out with her; We got along great in those moments. Overall, the bad outweighed the good in our relationship.

Today we have a much healthier relationship. We don't have the 'friendship' some sisters have, but we have a sister bond growing in some form. Truly this started since our mom's death in 2016, and even more so during my battle with breast cancer. She was there for me; I appreciate her for that, and I don't hold any past situation against her. I forgave her a long time ago, and I pray for her often. After my surgery, she came over at a time when I couldn't lift my arms to do much of anything, not even shower. My sister shocked me by showering me. She helped me out of bed and to the shower, just like our mom would do, and as she was washing me, tears welled up in my eyes. I had never seen her in that light before.

She helped me, and she didn't have to. That's love. That day, I spoke my thoughts out loud, "My sister does love me."

Her response as she laughed, "Yeah, I love you. What are you talking about?" With more laughter.

I realized that she has her issues. I don't know all of what her childhood was like from her perspective. I know what I experienced from my perspective, yet that day had me thinking about things like that. Wondering what her experiences were.

My younger brother Len became closer to Jade as an adult. When he was younger, we were closer. But as adults, our differences far outweighed our similarities, and we drifted apart. I found myself going further into a world I created, a new "me" because I didn't know who I was supposed to be.

SIBLINGS

I never fit in with my siblings or anyone around me. Maybe it was me? Perhaps I didn't try harder to build that relationship once we got older? To my credit, I had so much pain from our relationship when I was growing up that, at one point, I stopped trying. It seemed so one-sided. I started living my life and *doing me,* and they did the same.

Len stopped going to school at 15 and was hanging out in the streets with his friends. He later got his high school completion certificate. Len started selling drugs and eventually went to jail. I can't recall how much time he got, but he got out and was on probation. I remember when my brother was in the halfway house, and I bought him t-shirts and underwear. He called me to ask for those things, and I took care of it. Yet when they released him, I didn't know it. There was a lot I didn't know. He would call Jade instead. I wanted first-hand information from him like he gave her.

I was hurt and jealous because I wanted to have a relationship with him like that as well. But they were closer, so it made sense. They were both mom and dad's kids biologically. I was just momma's baby, and daddy claimed me. Len would always tease me about how I talk and call me "bougie" and things like that. He made me feel like I was wrong for wanting more for myself. My brother had no problem cussing me out or anyone, especially drunk. But then he would apologize to me, and I appreciated that apology.

He reminded me of Daddy. Daddy could sometimes say the wrong thing, but then say over and over when drunk, "You know

I love you, right? You know I love your momma, right? I love all my kids." And then end it with a dramatic "Damn!" or "Hell!"

I recall two phone calls where Len and I had long, open conversations. I remember them vividly because they were rare. We don't have deep discussions often, so these were significant to me. I'll speak on one of them because both were similar. He called and talked real to me, telling me what he was currently going through and some past events. He was drunk/high at the time, but I didn't care. We were talking! Besides, I didn't judge him about that because I did it also. My little brother was sharing his life with me. It was the first time we talked so openly.

I felt close to him in that moment, like a real big sister. It seems foolish now to be so happy about a drunken call, but it meant a lot to me because it wasn't something Len and I did. Our lives are different, and we don't run in the same circles as him and Jade. Len and I had to find other ways to connect.

I had to get to a place of acceptance. My brother is who he is, and I am who I am. We are siblings, and we love each other. We don't have to talk often, but it's all love when we do. I pray that they have both come to a similar resolve regarding me. We must allow each other to "be" who we are without judgment.

Today, the difference between my brother and I's relationship is a willingness to try. We are not functioning as we always have. We talk more.

SIBLINGS

My sister and I have progressed in our relationship since the death of our parents.

I know that we each have a unique perspective on our childhood, and I don't know what they have experienced if anything. But I do know that much goes unspoken between the 3 of us still to this day.

MOMMY

Growing up was fun most times with my mom because she made it fun; she loved to dance and play "dress-up," if you will. She wore skirts and heels and put on makeup as though she were going somewhere, but she was a housewife and didn't go too many places, except school.

It seemed she was always taking a class for one thing or another, obtaining certificates but doing nothing with them.

For example, she had certifications as a nursing assistant, a bank teller, etc., yet she didn't work in those professions. She even went to school to be an alcohol and drug counselor. The only job I remember my mom having for any considerable length of time was at a linen factory. Other than that, she continued to learn and obtain certificates of completion. She was in a vicious cycle of "stuck."

I never understood that until I was older and realized she needed an escape. She would jokingly say to us, "I'm going to run away."

My mom was smart and loved to learn. I am like her in that way. However, I don't want to be like her in gaining school certificates but not using them. She was a talented dreamer, but there was no execution—just dreams. That disappointed me.

Anyway, I would sit on the couch, smiling and clapping with excitement, watching my mom model all her beautiful clothes. She would come out of her bedroom with a beautiful skirt and blouse that she sewed (Yes, she sewed clothes as well).

I admired her in many ways.

One day I asked, "Mommy, why are you doing all of this?

"You are not going anywhere."

Laughing, she replied, "Tara, a woman should be well-groomed every day." She added, "I want to look good every day your daddy gets home from work."

She said that even if she was a stay at home, mom. She taught me that men were visual, and it's important to look your best whether you're going somewhere or not. She also said to clean the house and have dinner cooked when Daddy got home from work.

She did all of that; Laundry, ironing, and making plates for everyone. Daddy first, of course. I learned a lot from my mom, and much I do today in my everyday life with my husband and children.

She taught me that the wife and mother's role is particularly important and the nucleus of the family. We control the atmosphere; if Momma not happy, no one happy. My mom cooked breakfast, lunch, dinner, and dessert. We even had a vegetable and herb garden. She baked fresh bread, allowing the yeast to rise. I learned to cook and bake from my mom.

I still enjoy cooking to this very day. I love to see my family happy with my meals. She didn't work outside the home when she and daddy were together. She had enough on her hands in the house. Being a housewife is a lot of work. It seems as if it never ends. She was always taking care of us all day. I have some of her ways, but I'm not my mom.

My mom always danced and sang. She even rapped and read her poetry. It was fun at home with mom. She was a prolific writer who constantly wrote about love and the conditions of the Black race. My mom was amazing. I truly admired her at many times in my life, and at other times, I was disappointed in her.

My mother became an alcoholic. I don't know exactly when it started. Still, I remember her drinking Crown Royal in the purple bag almost daily when I was about 10 or 11. It was sad to watch a woman so intelligent succumb to alcohol. She continued drinking throughout her life, only stopping when she was deeply involved in religion or when she made up her mind to do so. I've seen it happen in both instances.

I watched Momma change throughout the years, and when she was under the influence, I didn't want to be around her at all. She wasn't the mom I knew. But I later realized she was unhappy with her life.

Momma confessed the abuse she experienced as a child and the rape that occurred to her as an adult. My mom didn't have the easiest life, yet she pressed on the best way she knew how. She was tough, but there was also a sadness there. I saw it in her eyes. It made me happy that we could speak openly about these things. My mom was so cool and transparent. She was the most authentic person I've ever known—even to this day. Most times, I listened to her advice; other times, I rebelled. She raised us the best way she knew how. I know that now. She drank so much that it affected her health. She would slow down and sometimes quit, but it always came back with a vengeance. It was her way of coping.

DADDY

This chapter was the hardest to write. Everything started with Daddy.

Daddy tolerated me. Growing up in our home, I saw that Daddy liked my siblings best because he didn't try to hide it. He punished me for any small thing I did. Yet, I loved him; he was the only daddy I knew.

I developed rejection issues because of the favoritism. I sensed I wasn't his child, even before my mother told me. I didn't feel loved by him. He was mean to me for no reason.

I will never forget the beating he gave me with the telephone extension cord as I crouched near the toilet in the bathroom in the small space next to the tub. Mom never beat us. She had us hold our hands out, and she gave us like five swings of the belt in our hands for punishment, and we knew why we were being punished. She would talk to us so that we understood what we did wrong.

What Daddy was doing to me had never happened before. I was trying to fill that space as much as possible, pressing back into the wall, trying to escape the lashes that continuously came. I don't know what I did to deserve that.

Even as I type this, I still see myself cowering in that tiny space, trying to escape the lashes. *Why did Daddy hate me?* I would think to myself; I didn't understand. Later I came to understand it wasn't me, per se', but it was what I represented, another man's child. Even though Daddy cheated on Mom and had two children in Mississippi, he still resented my presence. But that's another story, and I will not elaborate.

He and my mom argued about the beating when she came home from class after I told her. My dad was a gambler and had been all my life. Sometimes he would hit big. You could find him at card parties regularly or shooting dice. Daddy didn't discriminate when it came to gambling, but his favorite was scratch-off tickets. Daddy would scratch them all day.

Daddy had some demons that he was wrestling with, Alcohol and gambling. Sometimes he won, and other times it was beating him down. The beating downtimes became more frequent. He and mom would argue about bills and rent because daddy had gambled the money away. Daddy was a passive man. He was not a fighter. My mom said that often of him. My mom was aggressive. I remember her yelling and cursing him out often about his habits outside of the home.

I can still hear them now.

My mom would yell at daddy, "How are we going to pay the rent, Lamp?"

Daddy would curse and respond, "I will borrow it."

It became a vicious cycle. Daddy was a well-liked man, laid back, and loved to laugh and dance. He didn't have a problem getting money lent to him. People enjoyed his company. So, he borrowed money regularly.

To this day, I am not fond of gambling. Before we dated, I would ask a guy if he was a gambler, which was a no-no for me if he was a serious gambler. Addictions to gambling and alcohol were the major reasons that our household was in turmoil regularly. It brought the demons out. I've gambled at the casino, but I had a limit and kept to it. I had zero desire to take it to the max. It wasn't my vice.

Other things happened in my home, also. Daddy started looking at me strangely. He became more touchy-feely. Usually, he didn't bother with me, but suddenly, he wanted hugs—Long ones. I didn't like that because they didn't feel right.

At one point, he removed the bedroom door of my sister, and I's shared room, and Jade and I had no privacy to change our clothes. We started to go to the bathroom. My household was full of dysfunction. Some days it was the absolute best, and other times, not so much.

He and mom started arguing more and more. When I became older, I began to see that this is something that occurs in many homes. Many times, wives feel trapped, and children suffer. But on the flip side, they partied and danced with each other often. We would laugh and watch them, and sometimes join in.

One night, I was lying on a palette on the floor watching television when I heard the back door open and close. I turned my head to see my daddy staggering in. "Hi, Daddy," I said, smiling at him. Then I turned back towards the TV. Daddy had been in the back at the neighbors drinking and gambling.

He asked me what I was watching and if he could watch it too. "Yes, Daddy." I was happy that he wanted to spend time with me, and I said okay. My mom wasn't home. I don't know where she was because, by this time, they both were regularly drinking. It was an unhealthy environment some days.

The following events changed my life forever. Daddy came and laid next to me on the palette, and I could smell the liquor on my daddy's breath as his face came close to my neck. To this day, I stiffen up when someone smells of liquor and is speaking close to me, especially a man. I said, "No, Daddy, you're not supposed to touch me there." Slurring his words and hot breath on my neck, Daddy says, "It's just Daddy." I started crying.

This memory is very difficult to write. What happened next ruined a 9-year-old girl's innocence and set off a chain of events in my life that recovery could only come from God.

I became withdrawn. Everything went back to business as usual, but Momma kept asking me what was wrong with me, and I eventually told her. I remember saying, "Daddy touched me." I was so scared because I thought it was my fault. I thought I did something wrong. Momma always told me, for as long as I can remember, never to let anyone touch me in those places. I was scared. Why did it happen to me? Did it happen to Jade? When Mom confronted him, they argued, and he denied it, calling me a liar. I remember the yelling. He was lying, and I hated him at that moment. My childhood innocence was gone.

Momma told me my daddy was a sick man, that he wasn't himself. Daddy never touched me like that again, but someone else did. I'll speak on that later. Momma made Daddy leave the house. I think he was just like around the corner with another lady. I remember my mom started dating also and had a regular boyfriend. She was happy all the time until he went to prison.

But it was weird because Daddy would leave and then come back to the house sometimes. I think they were off and on. Daddy paid the bills, so I don't know what happened, but we left to live with Grandma.

My childhood—especially my relationship with my daddy— affected my outlook on men and even myself. What was wrong with me? That's what I wondered. I felt unwanted growing up; rejected. I wanted him to love me like I was his real daughter. I wanted him to accept me as his daughter. I called him "Daddy," but it wasn't until I was an adult that I truly felt like he was "Daddy" in my life. I say this because he started to be there for me as a dad. He helped me in every home with moving, painting, and planting my flowers because he was a Landscaper by trade. He started calling me often, and we had a pretty good relationship. I was ok as long as there was no touching. I talked with my dad and spent time with him, but I rarely touched him, and I cringed whenever he hugged or touched me. I was uncomfortable with that level of intimacy with him. However, I enjoyed his company; I loved him. I'll tell you this: Whoever my daddy was when I was younger was not the same man when I became an adult. He put forth an effort to know me and treat me better. I not only recognized that I appreciated it.

In the weeks before my dad's last days on Earth, before he stopped speaking, I was able to tell him that I forgave him, and I thank God for that. We had a conversation that was long overdue; honest, pained, and necessary.

I thank God for it because he told me he was sorry, and he loved me. He said it in his way. He said, in true Daddy fashion, "I was fucked up. I was high! Hell! You know I love you, Tara." And he had tears in his eyes.

"I know, Daddy," I said, smiling. And I kissed his bald head. "I love you, Daddy," I whispered through tears. It was the most intimate moment we had ever had. I had no anger, no grudge. I know that he had a monkey on his back when I was younger. I understand a lot more now that I've lived a bit. Knowing doesn't negate the fact that he had damaged me.

NO ROOTS

When mom left our home, we had to stay in my grandma's basement for a while in the Diggs projects until she could provide for us financially. Oh, what fun Grandma's house was! The POE family was well known in the Diggs projects. It was a safe environment for us to hang out even in the late hours of the night. Projects typically have a negative connotation. My mother didn't want to be there, living in her mother's basement, but we had nowhere else to go. People were constantly in and out. My grandmother didn't even lock the doors. My aunts and uncles still lived at home, and I saw my cousins all the time. My grandma's house was full of activity. I loved it! It was some of my childhood's happiest memories because of my cousin Monica, who was like a sister to me. We were each other's best friend.

Of course, some bad moments were traumatic, but I was never one to focus on the serious stuff; I would push on. I would bury it somewhere because there were times that I would lash out irrationally.

I had friends, but those relationships were bipolar. One moment, we were friends, and the next, we were not. I hid my glasses during this time because my peers teased me regularly. "Foe-eyes" is what they called me. I couldn't see that well, but it was better than being mocked and, at times, bullied.

There was always a fight in me. I was defensive because the other girls would pick on me. I took the bus to school, and my hair was long, and my mom would put it into ponytails. Almost every day, the girls would pull my hair, and they would talk about me and want to fight me. They called me "white girl" and said, "You think you pretty!" and I hadn't even said a word. I just wanted to be friends. I never saw myself as pretty—even though people would call me that when they saw me out with my mom.

I dealt with bullying regularly in school, with people not liking me based on how I spoke or my appearance. I started to adjust my looks and speech to fit in with others. My mom taught me proper dialect, but I tried to change it because it was too noticeable. When I would tell my older cousins about the kids messing with me, they would go to them and ask them to stop, or they'd beat them up. One time, there was a family fight—my aunts and cousins against the family of one of the girls who were picking on me. As a result of the bullying, I started fighting regularly. Even as an adult, my defenses were constantly up.

During this time, my mom started studying and was baptized as a Jehovah's Witness, so our lives changed again. The Kingdom Hall was introduced and became a huge part of our value system. This was my mom's attempt at giving us a better life, a God-centered one. Our lives now consisted of 3 days a week at the Kingdom Hall. I remember the pretty dresses my mom would buy me as we would go to Circuit Assemblies. It was fun.

My mom had become strict with us because the religion was changing everything. We couldn't go anywhere, couldn't celebrate any holidays or birthdays; It was different. Jade being the oldest, got the brunt of it all. She was fourteen or fifteen when she ran away. Her actions showed that she preferred to be anywhere but with us. Len was too young to have an opinion, and I wanted to be wherever momma was.

And because of her newfound lifestyle and wanting to give us stability, we eventually moved from Grandma's house. Our next home was on East Edsel Ford in my 6th-grade year of school. I remember we had a 13" black-and-white TV in the living room. These were the struggle years. We didn't have much at all. We were on Welfare and received paper food stamps and a check every month for bills.

I used to get creative with my clothes and make them unique for me by cutting holes in the pants and using household bleach to create a stonewashed look. I couldn't get the latest fashions, but I would still look nice how I put things together. I always like to do my own thing and rock my own style.

During this time, my mom attended school, but she wasn't working; we received welfare, and mom made sure we had food to eat. Sometimes our utilities would get cut off, but she would just light candles. Reading was something we both loved, and we did that often. She would make up homework for Len and me if we didn't have any.

I remember being quizzed a lot with random words in the dictionary. She would never answer my question, "Ma, what's the meaning of this word?" She always said, "Look it up," so to this day, I seek the dictionary and thesaurus. I love to read, write, and research.

We also played lots of board games. Even though we were poor, my mom loved us and took care of us to the best of her ability.

My mom had a lot to do with my love of reading and writing. At this time, I was in middle school, and mom became increasingly inactive in her studies with the Jehovah's Witnesses. Then she stopped going altogether.

By 8th grade, we were living somewhere else. Between 6th and 12th grade, I lived in 4 different homes—no roots—no stability.

Also, my mom started regularly dating. Most of the men she brought around didn't last; however, a few seemed more serious. They would help us out financially when they were with my mom.

At that time, I wanted her to concentrate on us, but there was always a man around. Technically she was still married to Daddy. However, Daddy was also dating other women. Daddy came around sometimes. They even had the same friends and would party together with their new paramours. Mom was also back to drinking.

If Daddy could have been sober and not addicted to gambling, my life could have been different. That was my thinking. Is that childish? It wasn't if Daddy hadn't touched me. I don't know but growing up, as I did, I thought of many "what ifs." I often daydreamed of a better life.

My favorite out of the four homes was Rohn's off Edgewood in Detroit. I was near all the action. My second favorite cousin Titia lived over there, and I was able to see her often. She did hair and would practice on me and teach me.

During these times, we had dysfunction, but it was our dysfunction. We didn't know anything better. I wanted a better life but didn't know how to achieve it because I didn't know anyone who made it out of the hood. I mean, there were successful dope dealers, dancers, and prostitutes, but successful entrepreneurs? I didn't see them.

I defined success as monetary.? I didn't see successful marriages either. We described a successful marriage as a monogamous couple. They were unicorns. The reality was marriages stayed together but mostly in name.

Mom dated many men, but Charley made the cut. Charley started as a friend and had been around for years. Charley loved my mom very much and gave her anything she wanted. He also was good to my daughter Tyler and treated her as a grandchild. Yet he was a heavy drinker, and during those times, Charley cursed my mom a lot, speaking to her in a degrading John.

I hated that my mom took this type of treatment from him. She did so because he financially took care of her. I knew her to be strong, yet in these moments, I saw her as weak. She could take care of herself and not deal with the drama Charley brought to her life. I would always think. *Why Mom?* My mom was intelligent; she had common sense and read all the time. She loved history, especially Black history, and biblical history. I didn't understand her mindset. I thought she could be anything she wanted. It wasn't too late for her, but she didn't feel the same.

Charley drank and got high off crack cocaine. My mom drank to cope, and I'm convinced she truly gave up. She felt this was her lot in life, and she accepted it and drank to get along. These were the moments that I was disappointed in her. She was too smart to live this way.

One day I asked her. "You could do anything with your life, Mom. Why you date men with drug and alcohol issues?"

"That's who's in our community." Wow, she said that everyone had something they were dealing with. She was currently dealing with her alcohol problem. There were purple Crown Royal bags everywhere, which was an indicator that she was drinking again.

Daddy was also around dating who was in the community. Mom and Daddy never divorced. It was interesting that Daddy would just come around with his girlfriends, and they all partied together. Mom never asked me how I felt about this. But eventually, as time went on, it became normal. I guess I was supposed just to move on as if nothing ever happened to me. So, I did.

Sadly, Charley died from cancer after they had been together for about nine years. Weeks later, Mommy and Daddy got back together.

WHY ME?

❦

I loved to go to my Cousin Monica's house because it was so fun there. At 11, my mom was still quite strict, and going to Monica's house was like a vacation. My aunt Joann, who was the absolute sweetest person, was rarely home, and when she was, "no" was not a word we often heard from her. Monica was quite spoiled; there was nothing that she couldn't get out of her mom.

Auntie had a wonderful job, too, with the IRS. She also had a boyfriend with money. Their household was quite different from mine. I grew up poor. Things were okay when Mom and Daddy were together, but we struggled a lot when she left him. But Mom made sure we had clothes, a roof, and food, The essentials.

Mom met our needs; however, we didn't get a lot of our "wants." I learned a lot from her during those struggle years. I am a survivor, and I know how to deal with a little or a lot. Trust me. As a child, I didn't always understand why I couldn't get a popular brand of shoes or clothing. I would use comparisons: "Monica has them!" I would say to my mom. "Well, you not Monica, and I'm not Joann," my mom would say. I say these types of things to my children today.

Monica got whatever she wanted. She was an only child and my favorite cousin. We were awfully close, and still, to this day, are close. She's like a sister to me. Her children call me "TT," which is short for auntie.

WHY ME?

Our babysitter was super cool and didn't care what we were doing. Of course, now, as a parent, I wouldn't want my children with a babysitter like that, but it was cool as a preteen. Monica was lots of fun and still is. At Monica's house was more freedom than I had at home.

Spending the night at Monica's house is also where a girl touched me for the first time. We had a friend to the family, a "cousin" around my age but older, and apparently more experienced in life, or a victim herself? I never knew because I didn't tell anyone until I was an adult, nor did I ask her. I just let her touch me.

She, Monica, and I would all sleep in Monica's bed. During sleepovers, we slept together in the bed or on the floor on top of a pallet of blankets. One night I woke up in the middle of the night to her feeling on my private parts.

I didn't move, nor did I say anything. I just laid there. It was strange, and I didn't know what to do. I was wondering why this kept happening to me. And she's a girl! *Why is a girl touching me?* I thought. I wasn't experienced in this, and the porn we watched didn't show this.

Anyway, nothing else happened that time.

I eventually went back to sleep. She felt on me other times, as well. Another time, she humped on me, first side to side and then on top. And this happened several times. We never spoke of it, either. Monica would often wake up in the middle of the night and go get in her mom's bed, so me and my "cousin" would be in the room alone.

But eventually, I did respond. My body reacted in a confused way. It was a girl! I truly didn't understand this. Nor did I speak of it. She and I didn't even speak of it—even after joining her in the humping. After that, every time we were both at Monica's, this would happen. Many times, Monica was in bed. How she slept through that, I will never know.

Around this same time, back at my grandma's house in the projects, we played hide-and-seek a lot. There was an area to the right of the staircase with storage bins and boxes. On top of some storage bins were many blankets. I decided to lay on top of some blankets and cover myself with blankets. That was my hiding place. Others would go in the dryer, under the bed, etc.

One of the guys playing with us, a family friend, was supposed to find us. I remember him lying directly on top of me, and he whispered, "I found you,;" yet he wouldn't let me get up. He started humping on me. You see, I hid in my grandma's basement on top of some shelves or something, where my grandma kept the blankets. I laid on top of them and used one to cover me. I then laid completely, still listening as others were finding their hiding spaces. I kept my breathing controlled, lest the blanket gave me away, going up and down. Clearly, it didn't work. I realized he whispered because he didn't want the others to know, because then the game was over, and I would be "it." He would hump on me a little bit and then yell, "I found Tara."

WHY ME?

I am not naming him because it's not about him. It's about me, what I've experienced through these encounters in life, and how they affected me.

My mind was all over the place like, *what the heck is going on*, especially with who it was. Why was he doing this to me? Did he do this to my other cousins? I didn't know. We didn't talk about this sort of thing.

But by this time in my life, I would just be quiet and let it happen. It seemed like this is just what happened to me, like there was a sign on me that said, "Touch me."

He told me not to tell anyone and hide in the same place and lay the same way next time. My dumb self-did it too. Why? I even averted my eyes when he spoke to me in shame, like it was my fault. This went on several times, with him humping on me. I don't know if he did it to "get off," but he did it a lot. I got used to it until I stopped hiding there. That was my way of saying "Enough"!

I wonder how many people go through things like this and don't tell anyone?

He and I never talked about this. Never—and we are grown now. He is still around; I avoided him, choosing no to speak too much to him even as an adult. But I have forgiven him. I don't know why he did that or if he did it to anyone else.

People are twisted in one way or another. I learned not to trust or put anything past anyone. Molestation is not new to my family and probably not to yours. It's not something we talk about. Because of my childhood experiences, I am cautious with little girls around big male cousins, uncles, friends, or other men. But to be fair, molestation can and does occur with any sex.

WHY ME?

TRAIN UP A CHILD

~

"Monica got some!" That was me trying to convince my mom to get me some birth control pills when I was 14.

Monica was having sex and was on birth control. Being older, I wanted some also. But she said, "no." She felt that if she gave me the pills, then I would have sex. She didn't know that I was curious and planning on trying it, anyway.

All the inappropriate touching had turned on my body. I hadn't had real sex yet, and my friends had it, and of course, my cousin.

My aunt used to tell us always to keep two men and a change of clothes in the trunk. My mom's advice was for us to date many boys, don't say "I love you" until you know what it means, and don't settle down until you're older. She would tell Monica and I to live and experience life first. Monica decided to settle down. I, on the other hand, was obedient to my mom.

As an adolescent, I was privy to conversations that I shouldn't have at my age. I got an early education. It truly was the way of life. I didn't know it was a problem because it was our environment and lifestyle. I learned about sex, drugs, manipulation, alcohol, and more.

You become a product of your environment, right? Even in Elementary school, I watched porn at Monica's house. She even collected money at the door on half days from school, so our friends could see the Porn movies.

At 14, I had a boyfriend whom I invited over when no one was home, and our kissing went too far, and I lost my virginity. It wasn't great. I didn't understand what the fuss was about, but I learned that it does get better after talking to my friends and sister. Later, I started having sex all the time.

In 1988, crack hit the streets of the cities in the United States. Fathers and mothers were leaving their families in droves for this new high. The first time I saw crack rock was with a guy I was dating. He had little baggies of it to sell. He would say how stupid people were to smoke it.

In my naiveté—or perhaps for a better understanding—I asked, "Why do you sell it to them?"

His response was, "They gonna get it from somewhere; might as well be me."

Frowning, I pondered what he said; I reasoned that it was logical in my teenage mind.

I knew people who abused the drug. My mom even told me she tried a 51, a weed joint laced with a little rock or cocaine. I watched families destroyed. I knew it was a strong addiction, and people would keep smoking it. With this being the case, many sold it as an opportunity to make good money. I dated doughboys (drug dealers) as we called them, so did my friends and family. Some of my family were actual dealers also.

Not only that, when you don't have anything, you're always looking for a "come-up." The girls saw the guys with money as a come up. I saw my aunts, cousins, and friends dating guys with money and telling us not to talk to anyone who couldn't do anything for us. They would tell the younger cousins that we'd "better not be out just having a wet pussy with nothing to show for it."

These were the days men had money holders and stacks of bills in their pockets, low riders with rims and the bass thumping. There were a lot of "hood rich" people. It was great.

Many of us "talked" to men way older than us. A girl in the hood can be as young as 14 talking to a 21-year-old, or even a 24-year-old; it was normal. We lied about our age too. I always went up an age. If I was 15, I'd lie and say I was 16, and so on. As a teenager, I had an adult boyfriend who was 26, but I told my mom he was 19.

I would have sex with my older boyfriend, and he would buy me things and give me money. You see, 'tricking,' which is exchanging sex for money, was normal. Guys had no problem paying. It may not have been an actual monetary transaction like when I later became an escort, a business, and money paid upfront, but it was a transaction. As a teenager, it could be for cash, gym shoes, jewelry, and clothes.

I used to be afraid to ask for money. My aunts and older cousins quickly put a stop to that. They would let me know that the men were not afraid to ask for what they wanted. How could that be so normal? I wonder about that now. To put it plainly, they taught me to be a hoe. There were many hoes in the hood. But we didn't call ourselves that. To call a girl that was offensive, even if she behaved as one. There was pride in getting money from a man. Sometimes men, especially the older sugar daddies, would pay a girl to let them perform cunnilingus on them. Yep, you heard right. I remember me and my friend sharing a guy because he would pay us both at separate times to come to his home, lay in his bed, and spread our legs. Easy money, and we would laugh about it because it was a pleasure for us.

And this is before I was a professional. But the basic narrative was if you're going to do, make sure you're getting a bill paid, or something—a transaction.

Women didn't take care of men when I came up. It was the other way around.

Later, we were living in a single home on McClellan on the east side of Detroit. It was a beautiful home on a block full of houses. There was a big, covered porch that I loved to sit on and people-watch. It was our nicest home to date!

I don't know when it started exactly, but my mom went from, "Where are you going?" "Who are you going with?" and "No, you can't go," to nothing.

As a result, I was all over the place with Monica. Still, my mom had become so consumed with her life that she didn't supervise me as she once did, But to be fair, I also lied about my whereabouts many times.

It was during this time, at age 16, that I became pregnant. I was dating a 16-year-old "pretty boy' who stayed in the mirror more than I did. Although, I didn't know I was pregnant until my sister told me so. I thought I had the stomach flu, and my sister whispered to me, "You pregnant!"

"No, I'm not! I have the flu" "Tara, I can tell you pregnant."

I got so scared. How could I be pregnant? Oh, my God!!

I started to cry.

The next thing I knew, I heard my name being called.

"Tara, come here!"

It was mom, and I knew that my sister had told her.

I walked into the room and looked at my mom's round caramel face staring back at me angrily. Her forehead had frown lines, and her eyes were like slits. "Yes, Momma," I said as my voice cracked out of fear.

"Get in here," she said angrily.

I walked in and sat down, holding my head down in shame.

"You're grown enough to fuck but not to look me in my eyes?" she said. My mom was very blunt.

I looked up at her. "I'm sorry, Momma, I didn't know." "Didn't know what? That fucking leads to babies?! Well, you're not keeping it. I'm taking you to get an abortion. You're going to school, and you're going to do something with your life! I'm not having it, Tara! You're not doing this. I won't let you."

I cried.

"Momma, I can still go to school. I don't want to kill my baby."

The next thing I knew, my mom and I—a scared, pregnant teenager—were walking past the picketers on E. 8 Mile Road. They were yelling, "Murderer!" as we entered the Eastside Family Clinic to get the abortion.

I'll never forget that day.

I was scared. I didn't want to kill my baby but didn't know what to do. My mom said that there were no other options for me. Momma had this idea in her head of what my life would be like and was trying her best to see it through.

We walked through the picketers shouting and holding up signs saying that it was murder. I was scared. I walked into the clinic, and there were girls everywhere, many young as I was.

I sat down while my mom handled the payment and completed

the forms. I was then called back without my mom to have the procedure. I had to lay on this table, and I don't want to get into it deep, but I remember the pain and mental anguish of this day.

Afterward, I was put in a room with other girls and women to rest and recover, given some pills in a small envelope, and told not to have sex for a few weeks.

I thought of my baby all the time. Would it have been a boy or girl; how would he or she look? But time passed, and life went on.

Consequently, my mom did get birth control for me after this incident.

I am thankful that the Lord has had mercy on me. He forgave me, yet it took time for me to forgive myself. One true saying is, "When you know better, you do better," or at least you should. (I didn't "know better" for quite some time)

Unfortunately, I started early. I believe the experiences that I had before age 12 were a huge catalyst. As a confused child, I began to equate touch with love. I wanted love and acceptance, leading me through many difficult relationships and identity issues throughout my adult years searching for love. When I did get to know the Lord, I couldn't believe He wanted me. How could He love and forgive me? I was a hot mess. I'm blessed and beyond grateful.

TRAIN UP A CHILD

SCHOOL'S IN SESSION

I left my mom's house for the first time after an argument when I was around 16 years old. The tipping point for me was my mom's boyfriend, Charley, and his mouth. He was over the house regularly now, and he acted as though he ran the place. He had his own home and wasn't even living with us.

But it came down to him or me. Momma chose him. She wanted him more than she wanted her daughter, which angered me more than I could put into words.

I remember the day well; We lived in a family flat on Townsend Street. My bedroom was in the basement, and I went upstairs searching for food. Charley said something smart to me about me buying my own food. Mind you, I am under 18, and I still live at home. I can't recall Charley's exact words; however, I can't forget the fallout that happened after that angry exchange. He and I went back and forth. I remember myself saying that he didn't even live there. My mom intervened, taking his side. She said words like, "My roof...my rules, etc." I was angry, and she and I had words. I didn't back down; I was a stubborn girl. I was my mom's child-headstrong. She didn't back down either. I said that I would leave, and she said, "Good."

"Really? Good? Oh, OK," I sarcastically replied. I yelled while crying at the same time, "You're choosing him over me."

That day my heart grew a little harder. My mom rejected me for her crackhead boyfriend was my thought. I was pissed!

This was a turning point in my life. I was no longer home under my mother's protection, and I went to live with Malia, who was best friends with my aunt Dawn. (My aunt lived in the downstairs flat from my mom)

Malia was an exotic dancer at the time, and she had a small son named Matthew. I was already babysitting Matthew at my mom's home because my mom didn't mind. We all loved Malia and Matthew. Sometimes I would even babysit him at my Aunt Dawn's house.

My aunt Dawn was cool. She was aware that I had regular company in the basement, and she never told my mom. She was my favorite Aunt because I could talk to her about anything. She taught me a lot about the world and people. Some were jaded because Auntie didn't like many people.

Now, I was a live-in babysitter at Malia's home, which was cool because Malia paid me $25 a day. I also used her vehicle—a black Probe, one of many cars she would come to own over the years. Each time there was an upgrade, most times, she would let me drive because she was cool like that. As a teenager, I didn't own a car, so it was a win-win for me.

I often wonder if my life would be different had I never left my mom's house so early; if I had just shut my mouth and took my butt back down those basement stairs. I think of this often—especially when I look at my children. I would never want them to leave the way I did, which is why I am extra patient with them during their confusing and troubling moments.

After that incident, I called Malia, crying, "My mom put me out!" "She is talking about 'good. I can go!' Choosing Charley's ugly self over me!" I asked if she wanted a live-in babysitter.

Malia worked unconventional hours, and so I was available anytime I wasn't at school. Since this happened during the summer, I would be available all day. Malia said yes and picked me up that same evening.

I stayed with her off-and-on during my late teenage years. When I moved in with her, I became a live-in sitter and was able to drop her off at the club and keep her car! That was the life! Matthew and I would hang, and she still paid me. It was good! She was only five years older than me, but that was a lifetime when I was younger. When I became older, the gap closed, and we became great friends.

Have you ever met anyone who lets you be whoever you wanted to be with no judgments? Only laughter and affirmations like, "Go get it!" I hadn't—not until Malia.

If you had darkness and wanted to explore it, it was okay to do so. If you were a freak, it was a "no-judgment" zone.

"Do you." That was Malia.

This freedom level was a new phase in my teenage life, and I received quite the education around Malia. The first lesson was that everybody kneeling ain't praying and not to put anything past anyone. She told me that I would learn about how people truly were, and she didn't lie. Even today, I put nothing past anyone. I don't care who you are. I've seen too much.

I had learned that already with all the pretenders I saw in my everyday life, even as a child. However, school was now in session, and my lessons would come quickly and intensely.

Malia was independent, strong, and beautiful. She stood at 5'9" with long, flowing blonde hair, grey eyes, a banging body, and more confidence than I had ever seen on anyone. She carried herself differently than other people I had seen in my life. Malia walked into power and was very aware of the effect she had on others. She also took great care of her son; he didn't want for anything.

It was obvious to me that she knew how to run the game. She commanded what she wanted, and she got it; I saw the results. She only dated white men with money—married or not; it didn't matter. She encouraged me to date white guys. I tried, but it wasn't for me—no judgment to anyone else. I just love my Black men.

I quickly learned that money mattered above all, and real love didn't exist. At least, that was the consensus at that time. She taught me the rules of the game. It was important to look good every day. From hair to shoes, everything had to be on point. It was lots of work to stay in character.

I learned to make a plan A, B, C, and D, and make no moves until your plan was in play. Don't let your right hand know what the left is doing either. Move silently, and don't break character.

I was being exposed to something different. Men and sex were still involved but on a greater scale. She did everything upscale. Not only did she look different than the regular people I was around, but she also talked proper. Proper may not be the right word. Actually, she talked like a valley girl, which I picked up on and began to emulate. Her lifestyle looked glamourous. I wanted to be a part of it. When I left her world to go back into mine, it seemed drab in comparison.

Malia was truly kind to me and freely gave and bought me things. She did this for others, too. She was cutthroat with men when it came to her money and could spin a story better than Lifetime or the Hallmark Channel. It was fascinating to watch.

She would tell me, "Pay attention and learn." And that's what I did. Malia was fearless. I looked up to her and was not ashamed to say so.

I paid closer attention to what people said by watching her. Although I went the wrong way with many things I was taught and did—things I wouldn't want my daughters to do—Malia loved me and always thought she was teaching me something to give me a better life. She came from a good place.

The sex business didn't stop because of a bad economy. It was always up and running. Men paid for sex, companionship, and to fulfill their fantasies during any economy.

Granted, we may have had to adjust our prices slightly, but there was always money to be made, like street drugs.

During this time—and many years to come—my god was money, and I served it well.

I got quite the education by living with her. Coupled with "sex 101," I also learned how to do hair weaves. I already had a love affair with doing ponytails and just playing with hair. It was a passion I developed as a child, and she added to what I knew, teaching me new techniques. So, my love for doing hair started as a child, but the sex business snuffed it out for a time. I wouldn't revisit it until later in life.

I received quite the education in my teen years. We went to the casino, a regular club, and my first strip club with her in Canada. It was easy to go back and forth at that time. You didn't need an enhanced license or passport. There was a club where the men were naked dancing. It was a strip club, but they were stripped bare. I remember partying there and a different club; we frequented Windsor often. The age of consent to gamble, smoke, and go to clubs was much lower than in Michigan.

Also, no one knew us over there, so that alone is enough to free you up to do whatever you want. Malia would take me out hanging with her and her friends, especially when I turned 18.

What stands out in one club is a white girl with red hair dancing topless for Malia.

Malia is putting my hand on a girl's breast, saying to touch it and laughing. I was hesitant when she said for me to do it, and she said to go ahead. Then she reached out and grabbed my hand and placed it there on the breast of the red-haired girl.

I had never seen her engage in any behavior with the same sex at that time. I'd heard her laugh and say that she was "bi for pay," but I didn't tell her my lesbian experiences.

By that time, I had already been with a friend of mine sexually for about a year. Initially, that was something I kept to myself. Later, I eventually told Malia all about it—omitting the rapes and molestations. Layers were covering that up. Honestly, I never wanted to think about it, let alone discuss it. But here it is in a book. (This is where the "Shaking my head" emoji would go).

Her world was so free, and that is what she was trying to show me. I could do whatever I wanted. She would tell me I was grown and could do anything, and when I was around her, I *felt* I could do anything.

Her friends and associates were different than people in the 'real world.' So, I call her world, and the world I became part of the "alternative world," and people not a part of this world was called "regular people."

Not too long ago, we met for lunch, and she said to me, "T, I respect your church side, but you still not regular. You are always going to be different, T." We both laughed. I *am* still different and can't "unsee" what I've experienced in the real world.

Although I have been saved and set apart for God, my character is still straight-up, blunt, and matter of fact. I can still see bull from a mile away, and I can know you're lying and not even call you out on it, but in the past, I would always call it out.

Today, I have more tact. Ha!

One of the times I lived with Malia, a point came where she said it was time for me to work and "make some *real* money," as she put it. I was nervous, but I said okay.

First, I had to get a cabaret license to be a legal topless dancer. They were pricey. About $250, if I remember correctly. She then took me to where she worked on W. 8 Mile in Detroit. It was a place called Hot Tamales. We called it "HT's."

Sitting on the corner of W. 8 Mile and a side street that I can't recall was Hot Tamales. There was a parking lot next to it that was normally packed at night, but not so much during the day.

We entered through the side entrance. As soon as we opened the door, the Bouncer greeted us, and music flooded my ears. Girls were dancing on the main stage, and there was another side-stage with a girl. Men were everywhere. It was exciting. The atmosphere completely took over my mood, and my heart started beating fast. I saw topless women giving lap dances and waitresses walking around, keeping the drinks flowing. *Time for me to get my drink on to quiet these nerves*, I was thinking. I enjoyed being there, but I was nervous also. This night was Amateur night. I had on a leopard halter body-con dress that hugged my 36-26-36 body, and I took so many vodka shots that did the trick—ShowTime—time to go to the stage.

"Next, we have Cherry Red making her way to the main stage," the Deejay announced as I made my way up. Earlier that morning, I had popped in some hazel contacts. My wavy hair weave was midway down my back, brown with blonde highlights.

Cherry Red was in the building, "Cover me" by Candle box, one of my favorite bands was playing, and I was ready to show the audience what I was working with. The club mostly played Alternative and Rock music. It was considered a "White bar." That's what we said back in the day, "White bar" and "Black bar" to distinguish the customers who came into the various clubs.

I liked the "White bars" because I didn't have to dance hard, just slow and sexy, playing on the pole and tossing my hair around. The "Black bars" were not like that; you had to shake quite a bit for a long time; those slow, methodical movements didn't cut it.

The rules were that during the first song, we had to dance with our tops on, and during the second song, we had to drop the tops, so I let the top portion of my dress down. I was too buzzed to care, dancing slowly and seductively across the stage.

Men came to the stage and threw money. What a powerful feeling that was to command an audience from dancing. Wow! I didn't understand the ramifications behind dancing at the time and the slippery slope I was on.

Malia came and dropped so many dollar bills on the stage, and more people came. It was exhilarating. So, that started my short dance career. I danced there and then started doing private parties off-and-on for a few years.

Dancing was fun, but sometimes it just felt like demanding work, mentally and physically. I had to wear stilettos sometimes as long as 12 hours a day. I had to dance several songs on the main stage and then move to the side-stages and dance before walking around to get the *real* money—personal lap dances. It was $10 a dance at HT's, and my goal was to sit with someone long enough for them to pay for several dances. Each song was a dance.

I had a schedule. The night was the best, but when I started getting regulars who would see me and pay for my time, it didn't matter when I worked. Unlike escorting, in the dance world, I had Black men as clients. Most times, guys would call me over. Others I went up to, "Want a dance sexy?" I said flirtatiously.

Whether I "felt" like it or not, I put my game face on and got that money.

I went to an older white guy who called me over. I started dancing, and as the song was ending, I heard him say, "Keep Going."

Okay, so I did.

Two songs passed, then three, then I heard him moan. *Oh, Lord,* I thought, rolling my eyes internally. I looked down to see a back-and-forth motion with his hand in his pants. I looked back up as though I didn't see. *Dirty old man,* I thought. He paid me $50, and I walked to the next guy.

It was all a game. Money was the motivator. But at least, they knew what I was, and I knew what they wanted. In that way, there was no pretense. I knew they wanted me to act like I wanted them. For however long I was in front of them dancing, they paid me for my undivided attention or paid me to sit and converse with them over a drink.

Either way, they knew my time wasn't free, and that was the best part of that industry. The men knew to come correct.

Initially, they scheduled me with Malia, but I was on my own once I got the hang of it. One day, I went into the dressing room to change, but I saw white powder on the counter and a girl sniffing it in her nose upon entering. I stood there for a second, and then I turned around and went to the bathroom. I called Malia. "They in here doing coke," I whispered to her from the bathroom stall. In many ways, I was naïve still.

She laughed. "Cherry *Reddd*," she said in the long drawl she used when saying my stage name. "You'll get used to it. Somebody is always doing something. Make your money and get out of there. Focus on your stuff." She was right. That wasn't my business. I got my mind together, went out and got some drinks at the bar, and then chatted it up with the fellas around me.

Most of the girls were not friendly. It was heavy competition. I was independent, but many of the girls had pimps. I remember a pimp trying to get me on his team.

"Looking good, Cherry Red," he said.

"Thanks, Big," I said to the large Black guy, who had a few of the girls working for him. "Let me know when you want to make some real money and have somebody look out for you. It ain't safe on these streets," he said, looking intently at me.

"Naw, I'm good, sexy. Thanks, though," I said, smiling and winking at Big. I would pile on the charm so that even a "no" was well received. I liked making my own money and not giving up any cuts, other than to the house and the DJ, which were automatic payments each shift. Yeah, protection would have been nice—sometimes, the guys could get out of hand— but that's why we had a bouncer. He also walked us to our cars at the end of the shift if we asked him. We were walking out with hundreds—and many times, thousands—of dollars. That's why having a buddy was a great idea. Walking alone wasn't smart.

I heard the DJ announce me, and I went up to dance and make my coins. I enjoyed dancing. I couldn't work that pole like Malia, who was the best dancer I had ever seen. Strip clubs not only had the best food, but they were our go-to for entertainment, so I had seen many dancers.

After finding a dance rhythm and style that worked for me, I got an A in dancing, but school wasn't over.

The Oasis was next in my schedule of classes. I remember the Oasis clearly. I ride by there often today, or at least where it used to be. It was on Van Dyke, just north of a 10-mile road in Centerline, MI. It's currently a dentist's office. The Oasis is where I learned the art of sensual massage; a Masseuse, as people often call it. This time I was more nervous than amateur night.

It worked like this. Once the client entered the front door, he would be in the lobby, and he would see the manager. There was a door connecting the lobby to us girls, but he couldn't see in, and we couldn't see out. The manager would ring the buzzer, alerting the girls that we had a customer.

Buzz.

"Okay, ladies, let's move."

Lining up, I looked at all the ladies comparing myself. *I hope I'm chosen.*

We smiled and posed. This was the part I didn't like; it was nerve-wracking because I didn't know whether I would get chosen or not. I had no control over this situation, and it made me very self-conscious.

I was constantly changing my appearance to see what worked. I had different-colored contacts, costumes, and hair that I would change into.

Some of the girls had their regulars, who always chose them. The line-up was made up of a mixture of white, Black, and Asian women. Malia had regulars. I was new, so I didn't have them yet. I went in with her my first few times before doing it alone.

She taught a course in talking dirty, which would make me laugh because I felt silly saying those things. It was weird because she would teach me right there on the spot in front of the customer. But later, it became easy. When I pass there today, I shake my head, thinking, *wow, what a life I've led.*

SCHOOL'S IN SESSION

The Oasis was a place with various scantily clad women wearing tons of extension hair, makeup, and contacts. I wore all of that. I was a mini-Malia, at least that is what my mom said. She told me when I was in my 20's that I was starting to look like her in appearance, speech, and mannerisms. I took it as a compliment.

Today, females wear hair extensions down to their butt and beyond. Back in the day, only dancers and women in the industry wore hair like that and full faces. It's a daily look now for many.

I dabbled in this life and the *real world* with the "regular" people as we called it. I had one foot in both worlds. I was afraid to give it 100%; Afraid of what I would become. I had a double mind, and I since learned from the Bible that being doubleminded meant you were unstable in all your ways. Accurate description of me at the time.

I would stop this lifestyle and work at temp services and various customer service jobs. I was never without a job; that's for sure. The money wasn't great, but there was honor in the regular jobs until the "regular" people started to get on my nerves, and I would go back into the alternative lifestyle. I reasoned if I was going to be putting up with their mess, I might as well put up with the john's mess and get more money.

Furthermore, I learned the art of seduction, acting, and serious manipulation in this world. I knew a little as a kid, but my education was college-level out in these streets. Everyone seemed to play games, and I'm not exaggerating. I didn't know how to turn it off, and it began to spill over into my "regular" world.

Later in my story, you'll see that I graduated with a master's degree in this lifestyle, and I learned not only how to make money but to convince other women in the business to work for me, selling their bodies and giving me a cut.

SEXUAL CONFUSION

I was sexually fluid, meaning I didn't choose a sexual orientation. I slept with both males and females. At 17, a female friend of mine and I explored each other. It started with drinks and conversations, asking each other, "Have you ever…?" and we began what was to become many encounters over that year. I didn't count her as a "girlfriend," but in retrospect, that is what she was for that year.

During this time, I became increasingly interested in watching Lesbian porn, and masturbation was becoming a daily thing. I was fond of adult toys and attended toy parties regularly. The funny thing about this is that I was invited to a toy party by a Christian woman after I was saved and not interested anymore. I declined the offer, but I was amused that Christian women have toy parties. "Everybody kneeling…" Yeah, you know the rest.

After playing around with my friend for that year, my appetite for women was increased, and I was open and, on the market, discreetly, of course.

There were two women that I could say that I had a "relationship" within my adult years: However, I've been with many women sexually. If I had to label myself and my lifestyle, it would be bisexual, not feeling like a choice was necessary, but loving who you wanted to love. I lived this way for almost 15 years.

It wasn't abnormal in my world and the people that I was around.

SEXUAL CONFUSION

One problem I encountered in living this lifestyle came when one of my girlfriends didn't want to let go. She wanted more than I was willing to give. She dated men, and so did I, but there came a time that she wanted us to be exclusive. We had a great relationship, and at times we didn't date men, just each other, but I didn't want a public, out of the closet lesbian relationship; I loved men. Confusion, right? It's like my music collection. I loved Too Short, NWA, and Tupac, but on the flip side, I also loved Creed, Jewel, Alana Morrissette, and Aerosmith, among other artists. This was my music. I didn't choose. I liked a bit of everything.

I didn't think of myself as a lesbian—even though I had sexual relationships with women. Isn't that the definition of being a Lesbian? I was in denial. I met many men and women who felt like me; it was a sexual act, nothing more.

But I did have feelings for the two who became my girlfriends; we had great relationships. I don't want to downplay them, as though they didn't mean anything to me. That wouldn't be right.

Want to hear something crazy? I was so out there that I used to call the party lines, fulfilling fantasies for others and myself. High out of my mind, calling lines in the middle of the night. Who does that?

I wanted sex. My body would just be turned on all the time, and I would masturbate anywhere—at work, in the bathroom, anywhere. This is not something people talk about, but it is a hard habit to break. You can do it so often that you don't want sex with anyone because

68

you're so good to yourself. I used to have dreams that someone was having sex with me and release in my dreams.

It was deep. I've learned from watching a video my sister had from Pastor G. Craig that those are demons that manifest in your dreams. They are called the "incubus" and the "succubus." Wow, right? Crazy stuff.

In my mind, I was a free spirit; Live and let live. My friends and I frequented gay clubs and drag-queen shows; it was a way of life. One guy that I was dating went to the bars with me.

Later, when I started to date my now-husband Frank, I thought he would join in with me as guys did in the past when we started dating, but he was different. He didn't want a threesome, nor was he interested in gay clubs or drag queen shows. I had never met a guy who didn't want a threesome.

When I was living this lifestyle, no one said "stop" and "what you're doing is wrong." I wasn't hurting anyone, and I tried to keep it real with everyone I messed around with.

One of the two women I dated started as a coworker and then a friend who came on to me. In this world, there is an unspoken language, a knowing so to speak. You can sense who is down.

We became weed-smoking buddies. I admired her class and sophistication. It's funny because she didn't like blunts. Ha! I did, though. She thought they were ghetto and preferred joints.

SEXUAL CONFUSION

I didn't have that class. That is in you, or it's not. I pretended to have it but wasn't raised that way; she was. There was just a way she carried herself and her affairs that was noticeable.

This girl was so put together; there was never a wrinkle in her clothes. She cared about that, and I didn't. I mean, not so much. I think I had more of a rebellious attitude. I was going to "do me" however that looked.

She was meticulous about the way she looked. She bought expensive clothes; A blouse here, pants there. She took her time building her wardrobe. The first time I went to her home, I noticed the cleanliness of it. She had four children, but they were older.

She was older than I was and had a man who did not live with her. She had beautiful white furniture and an immaculate home. It smelled good even though she smoked joints regularly in the house.

The first few times I answered her invite to hang with her, we talked and listened to music. I would notice how she flirted, but I didn't make any moves. I only observed.

She would undress and change her shirt and stuff in front of me. I would turn my head, and she would laugh and say, "you can look," and I would just know what she was getting at.

Normally with women, I was the aggressive one (I had a control issue), but she was in this case. We started a relationship and messed around for quite some time. She was generous and bought me things and gave me money, yet she wanted a lot of my time.

She was possessive and didn't like me hanging with other people. That begins as something flattering until I realized that it wasn't cool at all. It became annoying.

One night we were heading to hang out. I had come over after work and stayed there with her until we got ready to leave. I rolled a blunt (after hanging with me, she started smoking them) She preferred me to roll. I said, "Hey, Sarah, want to come with us to the bar."

She made a face and replied, "Let it just be us this time." "Okay, cool, but you always say that."

We laughed and smoked before we left to go to the bar.

She just liked us to hang together, no extra people. It was annoying but always cute; As I stated, I was flattered. She was cool to be around, and we had lots of fun. We hung out a lot at the Tipping Inn in Detroit on Mt. Elliot; it was our drinking spot.

I don't know exactly when it happened but, when I stopped smoking weed and making some changes in my life,

I realized we didn't have much in common other than smoking, drinking, and hanging at bars.

When I stopped those things, we stopped hanging out, and I was working somewhere else. I saw her years later, but we never reconnected. She was at an age where she didn't want to do anything different. She wasn't interested in God or in changing her ways. I started switching it up, and we no longer had anything in common.

The last woman I was with, and the more serious of the 2, when I broke off our arrangement, ended up dating my uncle. Even after she dated him, she wanted me to mess with her. I turned her down quickly—that was very weird.

At this time, even before they hooked up, I wanted to only be friends because she wanted too much, and I didn't want to have a public same-sex relationship. She and I had several conversations stating that we would only be platonic friends and nothing more.

I enjoyed the sexual aspect of our relationship and her friendship, but I was afraid of exploring it further. I also loved the effect I had on her. In this relationship, unlike my last one, I was the dominant one.

I had a twisted way of thinking, and I needed to maintain control in my relationships. Sometimes I did, and others, not so much. But overall, she was my friend, so I won't act like we weren't cool; it just ended badly.

I thought she and I could go back to being regular friends without the sex. We tried. She kept messing up with the calls and letters, trying to pressure me for more after I broke it off for good.

She would say she loved me and tell me that I brought this to her, and it wasn't fair that I was back away. She was right; one night of hanging and being drunk, I did bring it to her. "Have you ever been with a woman?" I asked her as we drank at the club. "No," she said and laughed. "Do you want to?" I wondered, intently looking at her. This is what I did. It was something about the chase. "Yeah, I do," and we went in the bathroom and made out. From that moment, we became secret lovers for years.

When I started exploring my sexuality, I sought after straight bi-curious women, not lesbians. There was a thrill in turning them. I thought it was fun, again until therapy and later, my spiritual conversion. I was after the chase; once caught, my interest would wane. Feelings didn't matter. Sometimes I was cold-hearted, acting like a man, the type that liked to play games. Other times I was sweet and spoiled them. I always felt women and girls should be spoiled.

MORE TRAUMA

At the age of 21, I was raped by someone I considered a "friend." This was the second time I'd been raped. He was someone whom I thought I knew well. We both hung out in the same circles. He was a local hustler. He knew how to make money and had his hands in many jars. At this time, I wasn't dancing in the bars any longer, but I was doing private shows.

One day he called me over to visit and see the home improvements he made. His house was the "hangout" spot, and he was updating and renovating. When I arrived and knocked on the door, he answered the door in his towel.

"Where your clothes at, Keith!" I laughed.

"Shut up, big head. I just got out of the shower." We laughed as I walked in. I sat in the living room, looking around at the improvements he had done. There was a bar counter added and fresh paint.

I talked to him from the living as he was in the bedroom, getting dressed, or so I thought. It was a ranch style house with all the rooms on one floor.

"Come see what I did in here." I got up from the couch and turned the corner. He still had his towel on, so I stopped right there. "Boy, put your clothes on!"

"I am—look," he said, as he pointed to the new carpet and the crown molding.

"Oh, that's ni— No sooner had I said that he grabbed me, and I couldn't even finish what I was saying.

He threw me on the bed, held me down, and he forced himself on me. He became violent in like a split second, roughly squeezing my arms.

"Get the fuck off of me, Keith! Stop!" I was pissed off.

What was he doing?

I said, "NO!" I cried, "NO!" I fought, and then I just stopped and laid there motionless and defeated. I wasn't strong enough.

He forced his rather large penis inside of me. It was very painful like I was being ripped open down there. I wasn't turned on, so there was no natural lubrication as it would be in a normal consensual sex act.

I was scared. I had never seen him like this. He was like a wild animal, like a crazy man.

Afterward, I was still crying as my body was halfway off the bed with one leg in my panties and pants. I asked why he did that, and he said to me, "You know you wanted it." He acted as though all was well, and it was just another day.

I yelled, "I didn't want that! I said, no!"

He just laughed at me, then he said, matter-of-factly, "All the women want it." "You want a towel?" I'm gonna get me a towel." He then tried to talk normally, like he didn't just force himself upon me.

I looked at him like he was crazy. No, this nigga is not asking me if I want a towel! He walked to his bathroom and came out, wiping his penis with a towel as I pulled my pants and panties back on my other leg. I had pain in between my legs, and my vagina was sore, so I moved carefully. He didn't say a word, just stood there naked, wiping himself.

I remember saying to him, "You just raped me, Keith." He said, "No, I didn't. You wanted it." I looked at him like I was seeing him for the first time, grabbed my purse ran out of there; he didn't try to stop me.

I left and never talked to him again. He was my boy! I couldn't believe that this happened to me again! (As a teenager, I smoked laced weed, unknowingly, and was raped.)

I cried all the way home and didn't talk to anybody for a while. I didn't have sex, and I even took a break from dancing. "Why the hell does this shit keep happening to me?!" I screamed. After a while, I tried having a normal life, but nothing about my life was ever normal. Who was I kidding? That was traumatizing. I started some self-destructive behavior after my little break. I didn't stop dating men; I dated *more* men and treated them badly; I drank more, partied more, and tried not to feel anything.

A few years later, I was walking in the mall, and I heard someone say, "Hey, Tara! Long time, no see." I turned around to see Kim, a short, petite, cute girl who was a great local singer. I had met through Keith at one of her shows, and we would see each other now and then. After the small talk, she asked, "Have you heard the news?"

"What news?"

"Keith got locked up. He in prison." "Straight up? For what?"

She said, "Rape." I made a face and said, "I'm not surprised." She then lowered her voice, looked at me, and said, "He raped me."

"What!" I looked at her. "Oh, my God, Kim! That's crazy.

He raped me, too."

We then hugged each other, and we kept talking about it and explaining what happened. It felt so great to talk about it. I hadn't told anyone, and neither had she. We both admitted that we didn't think anyone would believe us. He had raped someone who did report him, and he was in prison for it.

I thank God that he went to prison. I pray that he had a heart and life change, that he was reformed. When I think back on him and our "friendship," and his interactions with people, he didn't care for women.

There was a disdain there. I always thought he liked men, but those things weren't discussed openly at that time. But I thought he was gay or bi. I joked with him about it, but he would always deny it.

He kept a flock of women, but that didn't mean anything. He and I met during work, as many people do. You can have lifelong, lasting friendships from the workplace.

Unfortunately, this was not one of them.

I wish I had the courage to report him. I got tested for STD's and HIV after that and did so every six months for a few years because I knew him, and he was promiscuous without protection. He would brag about his penis being too big for condoms.

The way I viewed men was so jaded. I didn't respect them, and they hurt me time and time again. I didn't trust them. They said one thing and did another.

I've been physically abused and so much more that I don't even want to think about. But I'm still here! To the Glory of God! I made it out of the hellhole that was my infested, perverted mind and way of life, and I know that anyone can, if they allow God to heal their wounds.

I've experienced so much trauma that I didn't even trust God to work in me. I would say I trusted Him but was still quite independent.

Soul Ties

I had such a disdain for men that I dogged them out, especially after being raped for the second time. I treated them badly and treated the women nicely. But I had no love for the men.

I dated 2 and 3 at a time and was honest about it. I was single because I wasn't married, and I refused to be in a committed relationship until I met Tyler's dad. But anyone who tried to pull rank or tell me what to do, I let go. I was extremely defensive and became a fighter, and yes, I fought men. I was no one's punching bag. This escalated to unruly behavior in the streets and to anyone who pissed me off.

Each time I laid with someone sexually, I developed a soul tie with that person, even when sex was taken by force. There are spirits release, and they came to be with me to make their home with me; I was being tormented for years, and I didn't know what was wrong with me until God delivered me.

The Bible speaks of what is today known as "soul ties." The Bible doesn't use the word "soul tie," but it speaks of them when it talks about souls being knit together, becoming one flesh, etc. A soul tie can serve many functions, but in its simplest form, it ties two souls together in the spiritual realm.

Soul ties between married couples draw them together like magnets, while soul ties between fornicators can draw a beaten and abused woman to a man whom, in the natural realm, she would hate and run from, but instead, she runs to him—even though he doesn't love her and treats her like dirt. In the demonic world, unholy soul ties can serve as bridges between two people to pass demonic garbage.

Other soul ties can do other things, such as allow one person to manipulate and control another person, who may be unaware of what is going on or knows what is going on but for no real reason allows it to continue.

For a moment in my life, I thought I was losing my mind. I had the sickest thoughts and behaviors. I know now that it was demonic oppression from the lifestyle I was leading. Sick stuff because demons are sick.

They talked to me, telling me that I wouldn't find love. That I had to be the boss and the aggressor, so no one else could hurt me. The voices in my head were always there, and it magnified when I was high; they were loud.

No matter what I did, it seemed I was involved in a mess. I tried to be happy and have stable relationships, but they were often abusive in one way or another.

I have been hurt mentally, physically, and emotionally. The cycle of abuse just continued. People hurt me, and I hurt people. Sometimes, I acted so tough with people, but I was scared inside.

Many people have these experiences, and I think of that when dealing with people. I'm not quick to judge. Who knows the trauma they have experienced?

The trauma I experienced in my life shaped my thoughts and my outlook on people. My life consisted of fight-or-flight constantly. My relationships were unhealthy, and I latched onto anyone who showed me love and concern, like a baby to a nipple.

ADDICTIONS

The first time I smoked a cigar, I was 15. They were nasty but necessary when I was drinking because they boosted my high. I would drink Boones Farm as a teenager, and then it escalated to Mad Dog 20/20 and E&J Brandy.

I started with Black-and-Mild cigars, and then "graduated"—if you can call it that—to Djarums. I began smoking Djarums as daily as people smoke cigarettes.

Marijuana was introduced to me at a party at age 16. People were rolling weed into white papers, and some were smoking it straight out of a pipe. I tried the weed pipe, but it made me feel like I was smoking a crack pipe, and I couldn't do it. My brain wouldn't let me. Crazy as it sounds, it messed with me to have a pipe to my mouth. I hit the joint and started to cough.

"Go easy," my friend said.

At first, inhale, I was in love. I felt amazing! I had never felt this good before. Weed was relaxing and took me on a nice ride. I didn't think about things that bothered me. Instead, I thought about the universe, asked questions, talked about life, and thought I was very deep. The typical stuff weed heads do. Ha, ha! I didn't think of anything painful. I felt happy when I smoked it, so I started smoking it every day. Literally, I thought I would be an old woman still puffing on my blunts, but God had other plans for me.

ADDICTIONS

Whoever said weed wasn't addictive is denial. I used to say the same types of things. But when you are waking and smoking, smoking throughout the day until you go to bed, and don't feel the same unless you are smoking a blunt or joint, then you're addicted. That was my experience.

I would roll a blunt to be ready for the morning. I liked to smoke it halfway and wake and have the other half with coffee. I did not like rolling when I woke up. I had to prepare it the night before and smoke it a little. Somehow it was better like that the next morning.

One weird thing is that I never liked to go into weed houses and buy weed. I would send people to get it for me, or I'd get it delivered to me. Sometimes I would go with my smoking partners because most times, there was one, and the partner would go in and make the purchase. It was on a rare desperate occasion that I bought it myself. I started buying half ounces and ounces so I wouldn't have to go often.

I would go to my daddy, and he would go next door and get it from his buddy for me, also. I had a few people that picked it up for me. This was all part of the delusions that I had. I smoked it but didn't want to buy it. I wanted it delivered and convenient.

I had imposter syndrome. I didn't know who I was, yet I had an image that I portrayed to everyone. I started to believe it. I thought more of myself than I ought to have. I didn't want to be seen in the dope houses. Crazy right? But I wanted to smoke. When there was no one to get it for me, guess what I did? I went to the dope houses myself. Ha!

Most times, I messed around with guys who sold it, and they gave it to me. Or, if they didn't sell it, I would have them bring me some.

I had a few smoking buddies. We only hung out to get high. You wonder why some people hang, who don't seem like they would hang? They got something in common.

I drank liquor daily. My palette changed to include wine when I started to work as an escort.

Malia and I would travel to Illinois and Philadelphia often and be drinking while we drove. I remember one trip to Philly. It was early in the morning like 8 am, and we both said, "Well, it's happy hour somewhere," and started drinking wine.

Addictions run in my family—drugs, alcohol, and sex.

Weed was always considered okay to smoke in my community, and many wanted it to be legalized. I wanted it legalized, too. Now that it's legal in my state, I don't smoke anymore. I thought that was hilarious.

But I had another issue—alcohol, and this one caused me problems. When I smoked, I didn't hurt anyone except myself. I couldn't remember much, and I was chill and relaxed but also extremely paranoid. I never liked to smoke and drive but would smoke in the car if someone else did the driving. I frequented the smoke shops, buying blunt papers almost daily.

I was a problem to others when I drank because I didn't know my limit and would go overboard, just like my mom. If you would have told me I was acting like her while drunk, it would have pissed me off because I was in denial and continually drank past the "spinning" point. If you are a drinker, you know that point; if not, allow me to explain. When drinking, you will reach a point when you know you're good and drunk, and it's a good drunk, a good feeling. But then, if you take another drink or two after that, or sometimes just some sips, your head can start spinning and become dizzy. You may stumble into things or fall. People around literally are laughing at you at this point. You may even vomit, but for some reason, it escalates the high. At this point, sleep is your best friend.

Growing up, I started drinking early. Monica and I would drink at ages 13 and 14. We went to cabarets at 15 and 16 and partied with the adults. I smoked cigars, and she smoked cigarettes. We saw so much as we grew up because no one shielded us from alcohol, weed, and cigarettes; they did it all in front of us. We didn't do hard drugs, but we saw all this stuff around us. When you grow up like that, it's normal. You think that is the way to live.

Drinking was a part of our culture and a way of life—and

I loved how I felt.

But when I was drunk, oh, a new person appeared, and she was bold, aggressive, and very sexual, but also quick to fight. I can look back and blush in shame, like, oh my god, did I do that? Alcohol, which is legal, is extremely dangerous. You can drink to the point that you check out, and something else checks in, and you have no clue what is going on. I guess that is why it's called spirits.

I want to pause here and share a journal entry with you from the last time I was intoxicated and lost my memory.

Journal Entry: May 19, 2013

Something happens to your body physically, mentally, or perhaps spiritually when you consume too much alcohol. There is a dissociation that takes place. It isn't noticed until you come out of the drunk haze you were in. It's amazing when you think of it—the power of the human psyche. 'You' as you know and others know you leaves, and another 'you' appears. That is a scary realization. How does a series of events take place, and you have no knowledge of them? Events that you were a part of. Alcohol is called 'spirits' ...why you wonder? Perhaps a spirit takes over? Is that too farfetched? What actually occurs when you get drunk?

End of Journal Entry

Okay, some backstory. I wrote this the morning after my sister-in-law's birthday party at our home in 2013. I was so drunk that my husband and children had to tell me what I said and did the next day. I had no recollection of the events. And then I wrote those words in my journal. That's a scary feeling. Alcohol is legal, and it's the deadliest drug out here. And when abused, it can truly cause some severe damage.

Another addiction started early in life for me, Porn and masturbation!

With the porn videos I watched as a child at Monica's and all the different sexual things happening to me, I became interested in learning about sex. I studied them. Although I didn't have sex until I was 14, my body was touched inappropriately often and had been activated for lack of a better word.

I started to experiment with masturbation, which triggered something that stayed with me for most of my life until I allowed the Lord to deliver me. It's amazing what He can do. My thoughts were one way all the time, and now I don't have them at all.

Many don't talk about it, but it can become an addiction. I found myself turned on at the most inconvenient times. I would be working, get aroused out of the blue, and go to the bathroom to take care of myself. I know men do this, but women also do. It was getting out of control.

They may not speak about it. I realize I'm speaking of things many, especially Christians, don't speak of. My instructions were to be transparent and have these uncomfortable conversations. Name the issues, confront them, and then conquer them! I won't allow anyone to hold anything over my head. I walk in freedom. Don't you want to walk in freedom? Let's continue.

ADDICTIONS

I had all the adult toys and watched my porn and took care of myself. With men and women, I would incorporate toy-play if they were willing. I was in relationships that after sex, I would go to the bathroom and masturbate to have an orgasm. It was an obsessive, habitual thing that had a hold on me, and I was ashamed to tell anyone. It was too weird.

Addiction to porn and masturbation is not just a thing for men. I know a Christian woman who told me that she masturbates so much, she repeatedly breaks her adult toys. Now, that's pretty telling.

Working as an escort allowed me to entertain all my addictions. The interactions between the clients were most times, pleasurable. I've found that when you are into pornography, it is sometimes difficult to enjoy "regular" sex. You need something extra and dramatic, and regular sex became boring.

AGAIN

～

My identity as a healthy child was taken from me. Whoever I thought I would be was altered by the various spirits attached to me with each disgusting act of molestation and abuse.

After my daddy, the neighbor's son also molested me, and it happened many times. This predates the incident at Grandma's and Monica's house.

Our families were friends. He was not a grown man, but an older teenager who was at least 5 or 6 years older than I was. He was always nice to me and giving me things. He said we were friends.

I was over his house, and he started rubbing on my face and back, then my leg and telling me that I was the prettiest girl, and when I was older, I would be his girlfriend. I thought it was all funny and laughed. I was chubby and didn't feel pretty; in fact, I would throw up after eating by putting my finger in my throat to try to be skinny when I was around 10. He told me I was pretty. No one minded me being there because they stayed right next door, and we were all friends with each other. We often visited each other. There were card parties and gambling parties there.

It started slowly, innocently. As I think back, he was preying on me. He would give me sweet treats. He would pretend to be my friend. He would talk to me like I was his age. That made me feel good. Important. No one really paid attention to me except my mom, but mom had started drinking heavily like daddy.

We watched TV together, and even when our families were all together, he would secretly touch me. I didn't say anything. I liked him. *I would be his girlfriend when I was older anyway*, was my thinking.

Eventually, things escalated, and he did more things to me, penetrating me with his fingers and making me touch his private parts. This didn't stop until we moved away when mom separated from daddy. He was another one who told me never to tell anyone. He would say they wouldn't understand, and it'll just make everybody mad at me, and then he could get hurt too. I didn't get it, but I know I didn't want my momma mad at me or nothing happening to him.

I was often touched and used inappropriately, so much so that I equated touch with love for most of my life. If you didn't touch me sexually, then you didn't love me.

No one protected me. That's what I know. My mom did the best she could, but I was on my own, and I became weird. The best way I can describe myself during this time was a "nice nasty, compassionate degenerate." I would be kind, forgiving, and optimistic on the one hand, and the next cursing someone out and knocking somebody out in a fight with my hands or whatever I could pick up and use as a weapon. At one point, I walked around with a razor under my tongue. I was violent. I had to come to grips with that. I wasn't in my right mind. My sister would tell people I was in a gang, but I wasn't. Like attracts like, and I attracted people like me. That's who I was around.

AGAIN

We just had anger issues.

The extremes and the triggers were commonplace. I thrived off dares, and I wasn't afraid of anything. I loved challenges.

What were the consequences to those who hurt me? My neighbor went to prison. I found out as an adult that he abused a child. Was that my fault because I didn't report him?

These are genuine thoughts; it made me wonder about the other ones who touched me. I never directly addressed them, yet I wondered: Did they do it again to others? Did the family friend hump on other little girls? Did my dad do it again? What about my female "cousin"? What about the men who hugged me, and their hands would linger in the wrong places as a young teenager? Grown men! Ones that looked at me like I was a grown woman, telling me I was pretty, and giving me money. I could say so much…

As a child, I had no hate in me. I knew all of it was wrong, and yet I tried to reason it in my mind that I must have done something for them to do that to me. Why didn't I cry to the rooftops? Why didn't I tell m y m o m about the family friend? O r the "cousin"? I was scared because I felt it was my fault for letting them touch me and for eventually liking it. I was blamed and called names when I told that one time, shortly after my family was broken up.

All of this affected me into my adult years and created a needy, insecure, argumentative, confused, angry, sweet, affectionate, compassionate, forgiving, loving, generous, and highly sexual woman. 'In a nutshell, I was all over the place.

Yikes!

But let me tell you something. For all my "craziness," I never lost my optimism and belief that there was good in everyone. Even though it all, I looked at the glass half full and gave people chances. I loved people.

Go figure.

EMOTIONAL CHALLENGES

I started writing in my diary as early as 14 and haven't stopped writing. Now, I call it "journaling," and it is therapeutic for me. There were many times when I would lash out at people and have uncontrollable bouts of anger. That certainly wasn't cool. My mood shifted regularly. That continued as an adult. I was an emotional child who grew into an emotional adult, and journaling helped with that.

Many times, I felt like I had no voice, and it caused me to internalize everything. I constantly made assumptions and stayed in my feelings. I didn't trust people, yet I loved them. If I was in a room and people were saying negative things about someone, my response would be, "Well, you never know why they did that. They may have something going on. Give them the benefit of the doubt."

For some odd reason, I was *looking* for the good in everyone. It had to be there, right? Seeing that little bit of good in people made me stay in situations longer than I should have—situations where the bad far outweighed the good.

"You crazy!" I heard that being yelled at me from more than one man that I dated.

"Your mouth gonna get you in trouble. You can't just say what you want." Yep, several said that too.

"Somebody gonna knock your ass out, you can't be hitting and throwing things." I've heard this as well. I was a fighter. I would curse you out and hit you anytime I felt disrespected. I didn't need you.

I've been punched, choked, smacked, and pushed, and I've even been in an all-out fight in relationships. However, I was no one's punching bag, yet I'm no stranger to domestic abuse. I was abused, and I also was the abuser.

But these incidents, along with my childhood and the rapes, left me vulnerable, open, and exposed. I did not trust my decisions. I thought it safer to just not seriously date but to work as an escort. Every time I tried to have a relationship, something foul happened. Every time I trusted a man, they hurt me. Being with women seemed less stressful and better. I never fought my female partners. But I wasn't clear when it came to this, and what I wanted or how deep I was willing to go with a woman.

The confusion I felt further made me spiral out emotionally.

There was resentment and anger that I would suppress as I grew older. I realized the anger I had towards my mother. I was mad at my mom for making me kill my baby, choosing her boyfriends over me, and not knowing that people hurt me and was touching me inappropriately. She didn't protect me. Yet, in her way, she did by removing Daddy from our home. There was so much more going on with me, but how could I blame my mom for what she didn't know? I don't know, but I did. I was even mad at my mom because we were poor, and she was smart. I always thought our life should have been better. I had anger towards the person I loved most in the entire world. Later as an adult, my mom and I talked about this, and she shared her past with me. I had a better understanding of why she was the way she was. It seemed generationally; the same experiences were occurring, with slight differences.

Consequently, I didn't know I was suffering from depression until I was in my late 30s. My symptoms were getting worse. I was manic and violent, so much so that my husband at that time I finally received help, was threatening to leave me. None of us understood that I was constantly being triggered and didn't know how to cope with that.

Feeling I had no voice was a trigger for me. I needed to be able to speak and stand up for myself. If someone tried to bully me or take that away from me, I fought back. If I gave myself to someone in a genuine way and played with my feelings, that was a trigger, and I wanted to hurt them.

What I wanted in relationships was an authentic and reciprocal love with mutual respect. I wondered throughout my young adult life if that was even a thing? What I got was a lot of posers; People taking advantage of my kindness and pushing me back into darkness every time I thought I was out. It would get so dark for me that I wanted to die, but I was scared to kill myself because I didn't know what was on the other side. I believed in God, but I had no clear understanding of what happens when you commit suicide. I wanted to be on the right side of Him.

Another thing, nonverbal communication, although easy to misinterpret, became my way of communicating. I would text fast and long. I was called the "Text queen" by my friends. This way of speaking, especially when angry, was dysfunctional because my tone and intent were often misunderstood, and I misunderstood the same with others. I was a fan of this communication style to express my anger and discontentment because I didn't have to actually "hear" the other person.

At my core, I was led by fear. Decisions I made were fear-based. Fear of someone's reaction. Fear of someone leaving me. Fear of not being accepted. Various fears, but I appeared "fearless." No one would have put fear and Tara in the same sentence; heck, neither would I. Not with the adventurous way I approached life. It didn't make sense to me. However, this revelation occurred during my therapy sessions with Dr. Matthews as she explored my motives for various actions of mine. That reality hit me like a ton of bricks. I had to be honest with who I was versus who I pretended to be. I'm speaking as an adult, living, and loving, appearing to have it together. I'm thankful that I know that the spirit of fear doesn't come from God. He gives a spirit of love, power, and a sound mind. Before Him, my mind wasn't that sound, but it took honesty looking at the woman in the mirror before changes could take place.

I will tell you this: I was usually laughing, smiling, and doing something to help others. No one knew I was depressed. In those alone moments, I was left to be with myself and deal with my demons.

I liked to get high, so I didn't have to think about my issues. I just wanted to feel good, and I wanted to feel free! I felt bound to people, friends, family, partners, even my crazy thoughts. I conformed so much until I got sick of myself and pushed back. I would get mad at myself for doing things I didn't want to do. I did it to make others happy. That was the "wanting to be accepted part." I would say I didn't care what people thought, and many times I didn't, but it depended on the person.

It was like an angel on one shoulder and a demon on the other. I listened to them both at different moments in time.

I'm telling you, my childhood jacked me up. The wounds were layered, and the roots went deep, which happens with unresolved conflicts and trauma.

In comparison, the freedom I have now is unparalleled. I think back, and it's like I'm discussing a different woman.

To God be the Glory.

BALTIMORE

In 1998, when I was 22, I went to the Freaknic, a party in Atlanta, GA, during spring break, and I met my first baby-daddy, Tyrone. He was dark and handsome with dreadlocks, and by the time we were driving back to Detroit, I was in the backseat, writing him a letter.

There was no Facebook and Instagram, so I couldn't slide into his Dm's. My girls teased me. It was only a weekend, but I was all-in. I was adventurous and not afraid to live and try new things and people.

He and I saw each other again when he came to Detroit to visit me. I got pregnant on this visit. He came back, and then we decided to move together, but not in Michigan—somewhere on the East coast.

We got a map, closed our eyes, held our hands together, and put our fingers on the map. It landed on the border of Baltimore and DC. His sister lived in DC, so I wanted to go there, but he said, "Let's move to Baltimore."

Ok, Baltimore, here I come! I was ready for an adventure. My mother thought I had lost my mind. I had known him for three months, and during that time, I had gotten pregnant, claimed I was in love, and moved to another state over 500 miles away.

Well, it started great. Tyrone treated me like a Queen. He was attentive, kind, and respectful, but his true colors were eventually revealed after Tyler was born.

The first year with him was amazing—until Tyler was born. After that, he turned into someone else. I refused to tell anyone back home. I was trying to deal with it on my own because I had left home and all my family and friends and moved to another state to be with someone whom I had only known for three months. I was embarrassed and didn't want to fail at this. My mom had warned me not to move in with him. But I thought I was in love.

To make a long story short, he was on drugs and became violent with me. One day, he was having an episode because I told him I was leaving him, and he said he'd kill me first. This was the craziest relationship I'd had to date. He drove the car into oncoming traffic. The drivers of the other cars were honking their horns, and I screamed, "Are you crazy! Stop!" I was terrified.

You see, he was trying to break me. He said so himself.

"You think you're special."

"Yeah, I do," I would say. He would belittle me, and I didn't want him to know that it affected me, so I put up a brave front. I didn't understand how he could go from Dr. Jekyll to Mr. Hyde in seconds. What did I get myself into?

But even after that, he turned it around and had me looking sideways at him, but I didn't leave. Various incidents would happen, and I would just deal with it. He hadn't hit me, but verbally, he would let me have it.

Often, I would escape in a book. I loved to read romance novels and would read multiple books a week that I got from the local library. Dreaming and wanting the fantasy love life, I would convince myself that things would change.

The final straw for me was the day when he came home being erratic. His drug use was getting out of control. I picked up Tyler, determined to get out of the living room and out of his way. He came right into my face, cursing and yelling— about what, I don't even know. He then punched the wall right next to me and Tyler's head.

"Tyrone, you just gonna punch the wall, so close to her head? You could have hit her!" I shouted.

"I'm not going to hit my baby. I'm gonna hit your ass!"

He yelled angrily.

So now my mind was racing. I had to calm the situation. I didn't say anything else. He calmed down, and I started to straighten up the house and calm Tyler, who had started to cry. I played my role, but inside my mind, I began to plan.

I finally told my mom because now it was over, and I was coming home. He didn't know it yet, but I was fed up. Enough was enough! This was not worth it. I was miserable. I wanted to have a normal life after I got pregnant. Tyrone had proposed to me, but I turned him down.

BALTIMORE

We weren't a good match. I was sober now. When I learned I was pregnant, there was no drinking or smoking, and he smoked more weed than I ever could. I don't know what else he did, but it was something. When we first got together, we got high together. He used to have a container with multiple compartments, and it had different strains of weed in it.

One weekend, he went to upstate New York to visit his mom, and my friend came from Detroit to ride back with me. I packed my Acura with all I could and put Tyler in her car seat. She was only 15 months old when we left Baltimore to head back home to Detroit.

Rose-colored glasses broken.

RULES WITHOUT RELATIONSHIPS

Back and forth like a pendulum, I swung. One moment I was all-in and living on the wild side; the next, I wanted to go to the Kingdom Hall and try to save my soul. I was convicted with the way I was living my life. Religion had been absent from my life since leaving home, but now I was a mother.

I didn't like to be sober-minded because I thought about my life and everything that was wrong with it and me. I knew that God was the only One who could save me. I knew the Bible; literally- I read the whole thing.

In the Jehovah's Witness religion, we read and studied the Bible regularly. I knew what it said. I knew and could answer questions based on my studies but didn't have the relationship with God that I wanted—the relationship that would change my mind, heart, and ultimately, my life. The life that was promised in those words I read in that book.

When Tyrone was changing so tough on me, I was depressed and lonely in Baltimore, and one day I answered a knock from a Jehovah's Witness name Lela and her husband, John. They helped me immensely while I was there. I began my studies again in Baltimore, but it came to a halt when I left him and returned home.

Now, after much turmoil, I was back home in Detroit. I had already been a stripper and an on-again-off-again escort before

Tyler was born. (I just couldn't fully commit) I wanted to study with the Jehovah's Witnesses again.

I wanted normalcy for my daughter. She deserved better than what I gave her. I remember my mom doing this when I was younger, and our life was stable when she was involved in the religion.

I started studying strong with Mrs. Barbara, a Jehovah's Witness who was super sweet and studied with me for quite some time. This time I planned to go all the way! I wanted to be a Pioneer.

There were stages in the religion. I started as an unbaptized publisher, meaning I could go out in service door to door with baptized individuals (this was required for baptism). There was a baptized publisher, which is self-explanatory, then there was Auxiliary Pioneer and Pioneer.

The difference between those 2 was the number of hours you committed to evangelize a month. You had to record the number of hours and materials you placed with people on "The Field Service Report." There were other positions, but I won't list them all.

Mrs. Barbara was pleased to announce that I was ready to be baptized. I had completed the necessary books in my studies with her, and I was regularly in service. Mrs. Barbara was a Pioneer. She served over 70 hours a month.

However, my 2nd baby-daddy and on-and-off-again boyfriend since returning from Baltimore, Moe and I were unwed and living together. Mrs. Barbara said I couldn't get baptized unless he moved out or we got married. Those were my only two options.

All things considered, I wanted to get baptized because it was time to get my life together. You see, I finally had a real chance to live a "normal" life, but on the flip side, we would argue, fight, and break up so much that marriage seemed ridiculous. But by now, I had a 2nd daughter, Devin, so we decided to give it a go.

I was baptized into the Father, Son, and Holy Spirit and Jehovah's visible organization on Earth. I did this in April 2007, right after being married to my first husband.

I was happy! I did it! I finally committed! I was done with that old way of life. I was a wife now. It felt good that someone wanted to make me a wife after all I had dealt with in my life. It's easy to feel unworthy when you've had the experiences I've had.

I attended the Kingdom Hall three times a week and went out into service several days a week to hand out the Watchtower and Awake magazines. My goal was to reach as many people as possible to teach the truth of Jehovah's visible organization and save them from destruction.

My husband did not attend the Hall with the girls and me. It was not his thing. That was okay because he didn't stop me from going. He would question me and ask me why I believed them. He didn't think it was "The Truth." But we respectfully agreed to disagree. It was a win-win—until it wasn't.

I wanted to live right and be right. I wanted to be happy, and I wanted God. I went to service as much as I could and only fraternized with other Witnesses. I cut people off that I hung with previously.

To go deeper with it, I wanted to *belong*. When you're told this was God's only visible organization, you want in! I even conducted my own Bible studies with people. It was important to do the work.

It's a "works" type of religion. I believed that if I didn't do all the work, then I wouldn't live in Paradise, and neither would my children and husband. I worked diligently to follow the rules of the religion. I put 100% into it. I was a woman of extremes. I gave all or nothing.

I need to point out that if Witnesses fraternized with others outside of the organization, it was considered bad worldly associations, which was absolutely frowned upon. So, all of my friends during this time were Witnesses, and we spent time together regularly.

With that being the case, Tyler had not been able to celebrate birthdays or holidays, neither could she participate in other children's activities and sports apart from the Kingdom Hall. You'll recall, I had the same experience as a youth.

The way it was taught to me is, if I wasn't "witnessing" to someone, then I shouldn't be mingling with them.

RULES WITHOUT RELATIONSHIPS

In my opinion and experience, it's exceedingly difficult to be a Jehovah's Witness because of all the rules, which leads to many Witnesses leading double lives. Rules without relationship leads to rebellion. Relationship gives you a desire to want to please God; Rules, you do out of obligation. Your heart does not have to be in it at all. It's like giving because people tell you to, and not out of your heart, cheerfully. You can be obedient but not submitted. There's a difference.

You do what you want people to see for the optics, but there are hidden things you are doing because you can't live up to what they are asking. You rebel against the teachings and the system. Eventually, you may leave altogether.

For example, in a relationship, you are careful with how you walk because you care—not for optics but for the person; it could be for the level of respect you have, the reverence. There would be such an intimacy where you know your life is worth more than placing pamphlets and brochures, that's for sure.

I've been out in service and heard people discussing while laughing, putting hours down on the report, including lunch and downtime. You're not supposed to do that, but there was a heavy emphasis on performance.

Motives are important. Why do you believe what you believe? See, that's a question I eventually asked myself, but more on that in a later chapter.

RULES WITHOUT RELATIONSHIPS

Using my example, any proper response based on the relationship would be, "I'm not doing this because I don't want to hurt or disappoint Jehovah." But when you are just following rules that you can't live up to, your reality becomes a life of striving based on works, without the full understanding of God's grace.

I believed what was taught to me. I had heard it most of my life. My grandmother and mother were Jehovah's Witnesses. This runs deep. I hope that I can convey to you the mental depths of these teachings. Lines were blurred and being submitted to God was equal to being submitted to the organization.

The main thing was to be obedient to the organization. Staying close to them was staying close to Jehovah. That's how it was presented, with the organization being at the forefront.

In my opinion, that's who you're serving: The Jehovah's Witnesses Organization, which was the Governing Body at the helm. I learned more when I left. Read on to see what I mean.

If you're unfamiliar with this religion, let me share. The Jehovah's Witness religion is referred to as "The Truth," and that is what I believed it to be, among millions of people worldwide.

All the literature came from the Governing Body, who was the control center of the entire organization. They were referred to as the "Faithful and Discreet Slave," as stated in Matthew 24:45. They were appointed to "feed" us spiritually. With this in mind, understand that when you are studying—and even after baptism—there is much that you don't know about this religion that you're in, things such as the actual history of it and all the failed predictions that were explained away as "new light." You know, surface stuff, and in all honesty, that didn't bother me at the time. I believed in them. It was all I knew. And I didn't dare question it.

My point of contact was the one who conducted my Bible study. I met other sisters and brothers, but it was all very controlled, as far as information goes. If I asked too many questions, I would be in a meeting with the Elders. I did have some questions here and there about things I didn't understand, and they answered as best they could. Some answers still made no sense to me, but I went along with it. It was important to be compliant and obedient. It was "The Truth,"—Jehovah's only visible Organization on Earth.

I was told not to read material of former Jehovah's Witnesses who were now considered apostates for leaving or either being disfellowshipped (put out of the organization).

Similarly, I was encouraged to only read the literature they provided, magazines, and books, which helped my understanding of Bible truths. Because of this, it was hard for me to accept other people and their beliefs. My mind was shaped inside the hive. I had zero tolerance for different beliefs.

This was one of the issues Moe had with the religion. He would speak of his grandparents, how awesome they were, and how active they were in church. He asked me one day, "So my grandparents would be destroyed if they don't join Jehovah? (That's what many would call the religion; *Jehovah*). My response, without flinching, was a resounding "yes." "And that's why I can't get with it," he replied. And we never discussed it again. Later I would understand how silly I sounded.

In the Organization, we were taught to think alike. Anything outside of what I was being taught was wrong and demonic in my eyes. I didn't pretend to be a Witness. I walked it truthfully and pure. When I couldn't, I left.

One draw for me was the highly organized way things were conducted. Every Kingdom Hall around the world studied the same scriptures and literature each meeting. That was impressive. Of course, they were Jehovah's chosen people. He was a God of order. In actuality, it was a group of men yielding control.

I remember in all my studies in Baltimore and Michigan as an unbaptized publisher, and this point was driven home to me. My teachers would make comparisons to other religions and "Christendom," as they called it. Jehovah's Witnesses just *seemed* right.

Higher education and having a career were discouraged. Secular work was secondary to the work of the Organization. You were encouraged to be content with sustenance and covering but not try to be successful in a career or life.

RULES WITHOUT RELATIONSHIPS

We were told that the world was ending since Jesus took the throne invisibly in 1914, and we needed to be busy with the Organization, who was the mouthpiece of Jehovah on Earth.

I was taught a different Jesus; one that was a "Created Being"—the only creation that Jehovah made. Everything else was created by Jesus, and Jesus did not raise in the flesh. I was also taught that Jesus was also Michael the Archangel; He was fully Man on Earth and back to being Jehovah's Son and Chief Angel in Heaven.

I didn't know He was a Mediator for me and that I could go to Him directly without going through the Organization. This was my mindset for years, and it was difficult to believe otherwise.

In fact, I didn't know that I could take communion and not just observe. I had always watched everyone else and looked on in awe at the very few who could. Sometimes, I would be in a service where no one could take communion. Later, I was amazed by the *real* Bible truths when the scales were removed from my eyes.

Yet, even with door-to-door field service, bible studies, and fellowship, I still felt disconnected. I was doing what was expected of me, but I didn't feel any closer to Jehovah. I was hoping that the work in field service and living the way the Organization said to live would lead me to Paradise.

At this time in my life, I would go back to the Hall and then live right, but then I'd find myself back in the world. Vicious cycle.

RULES WITHOUT RELATIONSHIPS

One thing I don't fault is the people still in this religion. They don't know; I didn't. I had blinders on, and was totally convinced, and would argue you down. Also, there is the disfellowship/disassociation factor.

When you are kicked out, no one talks to you. Even if you willfully leave, you're treated as a disfellowshipped individual. If you're inactive, they would still try to encourage you. Inactive is just not going out in service and missing some meetings. I initially became inactive and later disassociated.

It's crazy because this can do a number on someone mentally and emotionally. Think about the ruined families. Mothers stop talking to daughters, etc. Look it up; I'm not exaggerating.

When I stopped going, my grandmother changed in how she dealt with me seemingly overnight. Our relationship changed drastically after I told her I was done with going to the Kingdom Hall. You see, I would attend Circuit Assemblies and go out in service with her sometimes.

I even lost my best friend of 8 years at the time. She said she couldn't stay friends with me if I didn't attend the Kingdom Hall. It hurt me, but I understood the mindset. Leaving the Hall was synonymous with leaving Jehovah.

Oh, it's deep. But my experiences with religion further helped me appreciate a loving relationship with God without the bondage put on me by men and their traditions and institutions.

THE FIRST "I DO"

To be clear, we weren't ready for marriage, but neither were we prepared to leave each other alone. Moe and I had a weird connection; I can't explain it. But I will try.

Moe and I loved to be around each other, and as teenagers, we spent lots of time together. We were best friends. I had never had a male best friend before, but that was Moe. Initially, he wasn't my boyfriend, but we had some sort of relationship. I dated other guys, and he dated other girls. We just spent time together, as well. We didn't judge each other; that was a biggie.

When Moe and I first met, I was 17, and we were inseparable. We met in the '90s at a graduation party through a mutual friend. I went to Kettering High School, and he went to King High School. My cousin Monica started talking to his best friend, and we would all hang together. He was at my house, or I was at his place on the regular. He made music and was often on his keyboard or writing. I rode around with him in his old-school car with the sounds bumping. He loved his music loud, which was the way the guys did at this time. Guys drove around in old-school cars with nice rims and paint, with the bass thumping and a huge speaker in the trunk. I would braid his hair and drink with him. He loved to laugh and tell jokes. He rapped and made beats. Music was his life. However, when we *did* become a couple, we discovered that we were better as friends than in a relationship, and we were both wounded with childhood issues.

Some friendships should remain just that.

As friends, we accepted each other, flaws, and all, so it saddened me how it went left. Since we had been friends for a while, he knew a lot about my life, and I knew a lot about his. We confided in each other. Because we were so open about things, we should have always handled each other with respect, if nothing else, based on our history.

Moe and I didn't exclusively date until I came back from Baltimore with Tyler, and even then, we began a relationship that would be off-and-on until we married in 2007. This is how we began: I ran into him at Eastland mall after returning from Baltimore, and we hugged and talked. He asked, "Why don't you give me a chance? You give everybody else a chance." I laughed. "What do you mean, 'everybody else?'" I said with my hand on my hip. He said, "You know what I mean." Then we both laughed. He always laughed. He had a great personality and was fun to be around.

So, after that, we started talking more and trying a relationship. Mind you, I just left an abusive situation, running from Tyler's dad a few months ago, and now I am dating Moe. I moved fast. I was of the mind that to get over one guy, you start a relationship with another. This one was going to be different because we knew each other since we were teenagers. Or so I thought.

Moe helped me a lot with Tyler when she was young and treated her as his daughter. We moved in together, and that was the beginning of our back-and-forth relationship. Moe was a hustler and made money the way he made money. I wanted him to get a job, and eventually, he did, but being confined to set works hours, wasn't his thing. We begin to argue about stupid things. I worked a regular job, and then I started doing massages. Moe would tell me to "Get your money." So, I did.

Our relationship was violent at times, even before marriage, but not to the point of what occurred later. We both had strong personalities and would verbally go at it; sometimes, it turned physical. I couldn't beat him physically, but my words cut like a knife. And so, we would break up and date other people. Regardless of what we went through, somehow, we managed to get back together. This went on for about seven years.

Fast-forward to 2007. As I pulled into the driveway at my house on the East side of Detroit, I found him on one knee in the driveway, holding up a beautiful gold-and-diamond ring. I was like, "How long have you been in this driveway?"

I laughed because it was cold outside, but I was truly touched by the gesture, and I said yes.

With that being said, in March, we quickly went to Toledo, Ohio, and got married in the courthouse because Michigan had a waiting period. It was fun and romantic, but we didn't have any family with us.

THE FIRST "I DO"

My mom asked how we could get married when we had such an unhealthy combative relationship. But I believed in love and my family.

We loved each other the best way we knew to love, and despite all the problems we had. Even though the quickness of our marriage was prompted by my desire to be a baptized Jehovah's Witnesses, we figured all would be well in our relationship after we were married.

Neither of us had been married before, and by the fall of that same year, we were struggling to stay together. And by the end of the summer of 2008, it was over completely. At this time, we had two daughters because Moe and I had a daughter in 2004. She was planned. I wanted another baby, and we discussed me stopping the Depo shots I was receiving for birth control to start working on a baby.

After marriage, a point of no return occurred, and we never could get our relationship back on track, but not from a lack of trying. We had violent episodes in our relationship before, but this took the cake.

It was November 4, 2007, my birthday. He took me to his friend's house who had a studio there, and we had a fun time. I even got on the mic and laid some sound effects down. They were hyping me up, saying my voice sounded good and all of that.

I was happy because he never brought me to those places with him. He kept that part of his life separate from me. But I also had areas I kept separate from him. This is the weird part I was talking about.

We were drinking and enjoying ourselves. Alcohol played a significant role when we were together. We left with him driving from Detroit to our townhome in Warren. I offered to drive, but he said he was cool, and I can admit that he appeared to be so. How? I have no clue because we both were drunk, but I thank God that we made it home because the car ride turned violent.

I said some words; he said some words. I am not sure who hit whom because we both had no problem hitting. This continued and escalated once we got home. We both had scratches and bruises on us. It became so loud and violent that a neighbor called the police. I was thankful because, at that exact moment, he had me cowering in the corner of our bedroom.

I had the phone in my hand, intending to dial 911, and he said that if I called the police, he would "beat my ass." I was scared because I had nowhere to run. Moe was a big guy, and he was in full anger mode. I had seen him angry before but never like this.

I watched him lock the bedroom door, and I was truly scared. I was like a caged animal who was caught unawares, looking back and forth, seeking an escape but finding none as he came closer and closer to me.

I was afraid to call the police, but at the same token, scared *not to*. And so, when I heard the loud, consistent knocking and the words, "Police." I was grateful, thanking Jehovah because he was about to tear me up. He yelled, "You called the police!?"

"No…no Moe, I promise. I didn't. It wasn't me. You see, I never dialed the phone! You see, right?" I cried, desperately holding the phone up so he could see it. I was so scared. I hadn't felt that type of fear since I was with Tyler's dad when he purposefully drove us into oncoming traffic.

The police came and talked with us separately. Yet they decided to arrest him based on my face. Moe was pissed because he had scratches too, but I was badly bruised and bleeding, much worse. If it had been the other way around, they would have taken me or us both, I'm sure.

In any event, I didn't press charges. I just wanted the whole thing to go away; however, the prosecutor did. Apparently, in these types of cases, they can do that. Moe didn't believe me until they told him. He thought I pressed charges. Heck, I was trying to save my marriage even though it wasn't that great, we were still married. I would say over and over to myself, justifying any negative situation we met, "but we are still married."

I wrote a letter to the judge explaining how things got out of control that night, and we were intoxicated. I wanted them to give him a break. I told him that it was both our fault, and I even spoke at the hearing.

Moe blamed me for his arrest and never forgave me. He took zero accountability for anything wrong with us. I didn't call the police, nor did I make them arrest him. I feel like they saved me that day. I shudder to think what would have happened.

Our marriage never truly recovered, but we tried one last thing: counseling. Counseling didn't go that great, but he did agree to it. We tried, and an Elder from the Kingdom Hall counseled us. During counseling, I revealed my suspicions of him cheating because he wouldn't come home some nights, and that was before the fighting incident. After that, he accused me of cheating on him. We didn't get anywhere with counseling. Later, on the phone, the same Elder told me that it didn't seem as though my husband was willing to reconcile. He told me that I had grounds to divorce him if I chose, based on his examination of everything.

The prosecutor also put a restraining order on Moe, and we couldn't be around each other until everything was over, which took several months and led into the following year, which was 2008. That didn't help our chances for reconciliation. That restraining order further pushed us to the brink of devastation.

After all the court dates were completed, he came back briefly, but it was never the same. Again, he was back and forth but not gone completely—which not only gave me hope, but it gave our children hope, too.

Shortly after, Moe became ill and had to be hospitalized, and the kids and I would visit him in the hospital. I would bring my video recorder and record their visits. He had officially moved out before his hospital stay.

Even still, he was my husband, and friend and I didn't like seeing him that way; even though our relationship was strained, we were still a family. The last time the kids and I saw him in 2008 was in the hospital. We visited as usual and had a great visit. He and I talked about getting our marriage on track. It sounded good, and it would take some work-but it seemed possible. We had only been married a little over a year by that time. He told me that he was coming home when he was released out of the hospital.

Now, this is where it gets even crazier when truth is stranger than fiction. I remember he called me the next day, and I told him that we would visit when the girls were out of school. But his next words had my mouth gaping open. "I'm gone."

This man told me that he was out of the hospital and on his way to Atlanta. Um, what? We were there the day before. He proceeded to tell me that he could die any day and had to go live his life.

He said, "I left you some money in the mailbox." Yelling into the phone in sheer disbelief, "We are married, Moe!" "What about the girls?" How can you just leave like this?" I was like, "Are you serious?!"

And his leveled responses (because he didn't raise his voice during this conversation even though I was yelling) kept being how he had to live his life and be happy. He repeated several times, "I could die any day. I'm dealing with a serious illness, and I have to live my life."

But who couldn't die any day? Anyway, when I got to the house and opened the door, I saw on the floor where he dropped the money and note through the mailbox opening in the front door. Did he even come in? The note basically said the same thing that he said on the phone.

He did leave $300 in cash, and just like that, he was gone. I was left to tell Tyler and Devin, who were currently in school. I stood there in disbelief. I didn't call him back. I mustered up the courage, put my big girl panties on, so to speak, and walked to the Managers office. I had to handle this with them because he was gone for good, and I needed to plan my next moves. I always muster up strength regardless of any situation, and I take care of it because I have to. I had no time to sit around, crying in a pillow. I had to figure out what to do. This is what I saw my mom do, and I modeled her behavior of keeping it moving.

With that being the case, I needed management to know there had been a change. I explained to them what took place and showed them my proof, the note, and money. They offered to work with me.

I went through the daily motions because life still went on, and I had girls to take care of, yet I was so angry and hurt.

THE FIRST "I DO"

The only time I cried was when I was alone. I remember sitting on my bed staring in the empty closet that was his, with tears falling down my face, saying to myself, "How the hell did I get here!?" I felt broken.

This happened in August of 2008. Now whether he left the city or not, I don't know. I know with absolute certainty what Moe said to me during our phone conversation, and he never returned to the home. That was traumatic, so yeah, I remember that quite well. Even more detailed than I am sharing here.

My children had a challenging time during this transition, and so did I. I didn't want a failed marriage; I didn't want to be a stereotype, nor did I want us to be over. I didn't marry to get a divorce. I didn't know anyone in my family who divorced, even through tough times. We said legal vows before God. This was serious. But it was over.

Tyler kept asking why he didn't tell them goodbye, and Devin just kept asking for him. She wanted her, "Da-Da." It was terrible. My children started having nightmares, trouble in school, and wetting the bed; it was just a tough time.

Consequently, Tyler became withdrawn; Devin was sad and missing her dad, and because of her young age, she didn't fully understand what was happening. She just knew her dad left us. She became angry with him for a few years, and then in 2019, her anger transferred to me, and she let him off the hook. My prayer was for her not to be angry at either of us but to know we both loved her.

I tried to speak to him about it, but there was a lack of willingness to understand the impact that his leaving had on me and the girls. He didn't care about the effect it had on me because he had moved on with someone else. But I don't believe he ever understood the full implications of the loss as a family and what it did to our girls. It was traumatic. It quickly turned ugly as he tried to separate me from the girls, saying," I didn't leave them; I left you!" That's what he told me. Yet he *did* leave them and didn't even say goodbye. He would tell me to send Devin to him, and he would take care of her. "Just give her to me," were the words he used. "You don't have to give me anything." This was in response to our child support conversations.

It could have been handled better; that's my stance. The first time they saw him was at Christmas the *following* year, and his girlfriend— a woman whom the girls didn't know— picked them up to fly them to Atlanta, where they lived at the time. It did come out that this was the woman he cheated with and left me for. But by that time, I wasn't shocked, nor did I care; my main goal was to get Moe to effectively co-parent with me.

After our divorce, I told him she needed her own room wherever he lived. It didn't happen. I never understood him not preparing a place for her, even when she was with him in the year. I am a stepparent, and I make sure my son understands this is his home. I don't care how often he's here. He isn't a visitor, and he always had his own room with us. I wanted Moe to do that for Devin, to show her that she had a home with him by giving her a room and a bed. You know her own space, a space that says, "This is your home also."

Her teenage years became very explosive, especially in 2019 when she came "out the closet" saying she was attracted to the same sex and proceeded to start changing her appearance to look masculine; we were dealing with that. Well, I was dealing with that; he was ok with it. I was not angry; I was confused at seeing my daughter look so masculine. I was having trouble with all the changes my daughter was going through all at once. I loved her but didn't understand what was happening. Or why.

On top of that, I found out she was smoking weed, and all types of behavior challenges followed. It was rough and challenging. I became the "bad uncool parent," and he was the good one in her eyes.

After an argument with Devin, she said she wanted to move with her dad. I called him, letting him know she was asking to go be with him. After blaming me for her behavior, he said she was always welcome. She then changed her mind. She is a teenager and dealing with our baggage and her own identity. She was playing us against each other also, being manipulative.

It's too much to unpack in this chapter. But the situation is not how I hoped it would be. I never thought he would attack my character the way he did with our daughter. It hurt and angered me. I even tried to plead my case to her and told her things about our marriage to explain the papers he showed her to see my side. However, that made me feel worse, and it confused her more. Both of us were wrong.

I could go on and on, but I won't. I don't want to spend a lot of time on what happened. But I wanted to lay some foundation before moving on to my second and current husband. Besides, the bulk of my life changed *after* Moe.

The most important part of our union was our daughter. I want her to have a healthy relationship with us both. I told her she never has to choose, and good, responsible parents would never make her. Unfortunately, her dad and I have had some ugly moments and said some unflattering words; I will say this: there are three sides to our story; mine, his, and the truth, the one that God sees.

In closing, after battling a disease that people die from every day, I understood better my ex-husband's mindset when he left the way he did. I didn't agree with his methods, but *now* I could empathize. When you are fighting something that could kill you any day, you want to live your life to the fullest, and if you aren't happy, you want to be happy. So, he did things that made him happy, despite who it hurt. Again, I don't agree with his method, but I understand in some respects how someone could do that. I wanted to run away during my cancer treatments and when my parents died.

It's important to know that I forgave Moe a long time ago. I pray for him in his health and his marriage regardless of our past. Why?

Because he is Devin's dad, he loves her, and I want him to be around for her. His marriage is important because she needs to see a healthy marriage here with him and with me. So, they are in my prayers.

There is pain in my baby girl's heart that I am trusting God to heal. She struggles even today, at the age of fifteen, with what occurred between her dad and me. Recently we talked, and she told me she doesn't forgive me for divorcing him. That shocked and hurt me. *It took 2,* I said through tears. I told her that I hoped we could work through it and get to a better place, and I apologized for hurting her. So, that is something we are still working through. In fact, she's been to therapy to help her sort out everything, especially her anger issues. The last few years have been rough.

Her dad and I must be careful how we handle each other, for her sake. But I had no clue this would be such an issue. I'm reading a lot about children from divorced homes and the impact it has on them. It's psychologically damaging, and divorced parents should never put children in the middle or put one parent against the other.

Although still a work in progress, through all the turmoil, miscommunication, and anger, we are learning to co-parent in a healthy way with better communication concerning our daughter, for the sake of her, because she is who's important.

For that, I am grateful.

OPPOSITES ATTRACT

I stopped going to the Hall completely and went back into the world after my first husband's separation. The world welcomed me back with open arms, like the father to the prodigal son. This time, I had no intention of going anywhere to worship. My mindset was to live, enjoy life, love people, and try to be a good citizen.

Through many studies, I learned that because of oppressive religious sects, many people leave them and become atheists or stay home and cultivate their relationship apart from organized religions. I planned on living like the latter group. Amid this new me, I started dating my current husband, Frank.

My intentions were just to hang out and have sex with Frank as a homey lover friend. I did not want to be committed to another person—I was done.

By this time, the level of hurt I'd experienced had me so jaded; I didn't believe true happiness in a relationship existed. I realized everything Malia used to tell me was true. *Why did I keep trying love and relationships?* I asked myself.

Anyway, my thinking at that time was, "Got to get that money." I had to take care of my children and working in customer service wasn't cutting it.

Such a huge change in my life took place in my relationship and subsequent marriage to Frank. I have never dated anyone like him. Even though I had prior relationships and a marriage, this was the most profound relationship that I ever had.

It was often difficult because it started and progressed quickly, and we truly didn't know each other. But it's amazing what the Lord can teach us through relationships if we care to pay attention, endure, repent, and turn to Him.

Let me briefly share our love story. I attended a cabaret in September of 2008, a month after my first husband had left me. I walked into the venue with my sister and friends, scanning the room; the music was loud, you could see people on the dance floor and others with their drink in hand standing around rocking to the music. Smoking inside cabaret halls was a normal occurrence, and the atmosphere was thick with cigars, cigarettes, and marijuana smoke.

I focused on the table in front of me, where three men were standing—one of whom was Frank—and I heard someone say, "Isn't that Tara? Aww, man." I smiled.

I had on a black, form-fitting dress that stopped at my mid-thigh with tall, thigh-high pant-leather boots, and my long hair weave was cascading to my lower back in black waves. I felt sexy! I *was* sexy, and I knew it!

Frank was looking straight at me, and we locked eyes the entire way as I walked towards the table! My mindset was like *no relationship for me, just fun.* I couldn't deal with another relationship after my failed marriage.

"Hey, Frank, it's been a long time," I said, seductively smiling at him.

He looked mesmerized and told me how good I looked as we hugged. We became inseparable all night. I had an amazing time that night, drinking and dancing with Frank.

I whispered to him, "I'm giving you some tonight. It's long overdue." You see, I hadn't had sex in many months. My husband and I stopped sleeping together when I refused to have sex with him without a condom. I didn't trust him because he stayed out so much. His answer was to stay out more.

Frank laughed at me, then smiled and said how blunt I was. I was serious; I was my momma's child! That night, I went to his house. Our very first date was at breakfast the next morning.

We became inseparable. Technically, I was still married but separated. I hadn't started divorce proceedings yet—to Frank's mother's disdain. She didn't care for me right away, and I understood. I was older than Frank by three years and married with two children. When we met, she asked me, "What do you want with my son?" Today we have a great relationship. But I digress.

I justified my relationship with Frank within myself because of the current situation I was in. I knew I would be divorced soon.

OPPOSITES ATTRACT

Frank and I had known each other for years. Initially, I met Frank on July 18, 2004, at my sister's birthday party, where I met many of her coworkers. Frank was her coworker at that time.

We didn't talk—other than to be introduced and say hello. Over that year and the following years, we would run into each other at cabarets and clubs. I would go to the cabarets that he and his friends put on with my sister; he and I would always dance together. Frank is a great dancer, and I loved his moves. We flirted with each other. Who knew we would date and marry? God knew!

An attraction began to grow between us both, yet we didn't initially act on it. The crazy thing is we were never single at the same time. Either he was involved, or I was. He was back and forth with his son's mother, and I was in a relationship with my former husband off and on.

We danced together at the cabarets, and I loved being around him. Frank was very cool, laid back, and lots of fun. He reminded me of the good parts of my daddy. The dancing he and Mom would often do. Frank and I only talked when we saw each other; we didn't exchange numbers for years. I was living my life, and he was living his.

Fast forward back to the end of 2008, when we begin dating for the first time. Once we started to date, I learned more about Frank. I realized he was calm and focused. He loved to drink and socialize. He didn't like to argue, nor did he start drama. Also, I noticed that Frank would keep his son on the weekends, and I wouldn't go over on those weekends because it was Daddy-son time. He was serious about his parenting. He shut everything down and focused on his son. I loved that he was an attentive dad.

We agreed that our first time introducing everyone would be a group meeting and date. With that being the case, we set up a movie and dinner date, and I brought the girls to Frank's home. Deonta' was just the cutest! He was only two at the time.

The date went well, and after that, our relationship took off! Everything was great, but I wasn't used to a man like him. He was incredibly open, honest, hard-working, kind, had, and wasn't hustling or cheating on me. He was attentive to his mother, but not a momma's boy, although he loved and respected his mother and her advice.

He was quite inquisitive and would look intently at me and ask questions. He had the kindest eyes I'd ever seen. Sometimes, I would just stare at him. And he would look up and smile and say, "What, Beautiful? What are you looking at me for?" He affectionately calls me "Beautiful."

Frank wanted to know *everything*, and I wasn't used to answering all the questions he asked; it was exhausting and uncomfortable. I didn't question him, but he didn't care. I dealt with him as I had with anyone, especially back in the day; I barely questioned anybody because I didn't want them asking me questions.

But on the flip side, Frank even asked about my day and shared what had happened during his. He cared. I would compare him to my ex—who didn't ask about my day, and we barely talked, especially after we got married. That may not sound like much to you, but it was new to me. I was eating it up! *This is great*, I thought.

He told me about his life and wanted this open and honest relationship. I was perplexed. I knew it sounded reasonable, but I was used to games in my dealings with the opposite sex. Even a "committed" relationship didn't last, so I wasn't too optimistic, and I am an optimistic person.

My brows frowning and head cocked to the side, I would contemplate this man. What did he *really* want with me? Did he like me for me? Did he **know** me? And why is he questioning me so much?!

I just wanted to make love to him and enjoy his presence. He was amazing in bed, and that was important to me. We partied often, and I had never had so much fun in any earlier relationship.

Okay, so talk about different. Boy, oh, boy, was Frank different. My intentions were not to get deep with Frank, and when I felt myself falling for him, I went to talk with my sister to ask her what she thought, since she had been working with him for years.

I wanted to know whether he was someone who spread themselves thin in the plant or not. What was the real story? People spend more time at work than they do at home, so I was curious about her perception of him.

"Frank don't do none of that. He's a good guy," Jade said. She then added, "He may be too nice for you, Tara. You not used to a guy like him."

I paused to reflect on that. *Maybe I needed a nice guy?*

"We will see where this goes," I said.

Months later, I remember my friend and neighbor, Angela walked up to me outside our home and said, "Tara, God told me that Frank is going to be your husband."

"Uh, no, because I'm not getting married again. We're just hanging out and having fun, like a homie-lover-friend type of thing," I replied, laughing. I wasn't trying to go there! "Besides, why would God tell you that? He didn't tell me that," I added. But I was joking. God didn't tell me anything; at least I wasn't aware because I didn't yet know His voice. Angela said that He speaks to her. She stood firm on what she'd said.

As the relationship progressed, we never wanted to be apart. He would come over and stay for the weekend, and I hated it when he left and went back to his home. We talked every day throughout the day.

Eventually, we were at a point of deciding whether I should move into his home on the west side of Detroit or if he should move into mine in the suburbs. He said he didn't want to disrupt the routine of the girls and their schooling.

After about seven months, we both decided it was best for him to move in with me. So, he moved into the townhome that I had previously shared with my husband. We eventually left there and moved into a place of our own for a fresh start.

When Frank moved into my townhome, I enrolled in hair school. I decided that I would pursue a passion of mine that was laying doormat. This was exciting but taxing at the same time being back in school. I appreciated Frank being home. He worked mornings, and I attended school through the week in the evenings and on Saturday mornings. This went on for two years because I was a part-time student.

Our relationship started so fun, and I didn't think he needed to know the ins and outs of what I currently did for a living or my past lesbian activity, and so I kept that from him. I wanted to enjoy our "now" and look towards the future.

He was the first guy I dated whom I regularly went out and hung with. We danced and always enjoyed each other. He treated me well, and I just loved to show him affection. I wanted to show him that I loved him, and the only way I knew was through physical touch, so I touched him often.

He said that he wasn't used to the type of attention I gave him. We became friends with each conversation, and in his arms was my favorite place because when he wrapped his arms around me, I would relax and melt, like lying down in a comfortable bed with the best mattress and pillow money can buy.

Even though we had sex first, our relationship evolved into something not sexually dominant, which confused me. I would accuse him of not wanting me or cheating if we didn't have sex regularly. I was tripping, I know. You see, I had to learn that I could be loved without the main thing being physical. He taught me that. That was another layer being removed.

He was a homebody and didn't like to leave the house too much on the flip side. I'm not exaggerating. In the beginning, this was comforting to me. I was used to someone who was always gone from home, so Frank was a welcome change. He would go to work and go home and stay there.

He preferred his friends to come over versus him going to their house. His favorite pastime is playing his Xbox video game. It did not bother me at first because he was home. He would say that to me. "At least you know where I am." This was true.

I, on the other hand, left the house quite often, which he didn't like. I loved lunches with my girls, visiting friends, taking my daughters out, or just what I call "be-bopping." Frank wanted us to move as a family and do everything together. I believe that we still needed to do things together but not all the time. However, I changed this part of myself for a time and stayed in as much as possible. I'm not a homebody— although I do enjoy being home.

I found myself trying to be what he wanted—but my mouth was reckless. I was loud, sarcastic, honest, blunt, opinionated, and a fighter. Also, I didn't trust men, and he was on the receiving end of that.

Frank didn't like that. He was extremely analytical. He knew why everyone did everything. I didn't like that. When he made up his mind about something, that is what it was. I tried my best to tame my tongue, but only God could do that. What a pair we were! Acting was over, and all truth was being exposed.

I thought we wouldn't make it because as the haze of partying wore off and reality set in, we were faced with each other, and we didn't know each other very well. We yelled and argued, often saying how the other *changed*, but actually, we were learning who we were. At 32 and 29, we both lived apart longer than we were together. However, we both did a lot of growing in our relationship.

Frank had trust issues; he admitted that, and so, he held on tightly. My trust issues didn't make me hold on; it made me hold a part of me behind lock and key. We both had emotional baggage from our childhood and earlier relationships. We both confided in each other about our childhood pains, and it helped us understand the other—although *understanding* didn't stop the painful processes that we went through. Each trial chipped off pride and added humility and grace.

OPPOSITES ATTRACT

The best way to explain "us" during this time is that when it was bad, it was *really* bad, and when it was good, it was *really* good. There were extremes like that.

Our relationship was like a whirlwind; it went fast, which was sometimes an issue; although we spent lots of time together, it was hanging out and drinking whether at clubs, cabarets, or home.

I smoked my weed and cigars daily, and Frank smoked his cigarettes. We drank and had sex regularly; we enjoyed each other. Our sex life was full of passion. It was spiritual—certainly a new experience for me. However, it left me vulnerable and exposed. It wasn't just a physical connection that he and I had. He got in my head, and those walls around my heart that I created came tumbling down.

In this relationship, I became dependent on the acceptance that he gave me and the security that I felt. Honestly, I didn't want him to leave me. I hadn't had this before, so I adjusted to please him, but sometimes it backfired, and I would protest in frustration. The result was an argument or silence.

I was still trying to figure out who I was. I thought I knew, but I didn't discover who I was until I started truly walking with God; I can say the same for my husband. Our challenges were meant for us to see ourselves. I had never had to see myself this thoroughly with any other relationship. God shined a light upon us and sat us in front of our own mirrors to face ourselves.

But even through all of that, Frank was a good guy, with a huge heart, who loved me unlike I've ever been loved in any relationship, which is what was tripping me up. I struggled with receiving it because it was foreign to me.

With his ability to "see" me often, he saw that what I did was not who I was. He said he saw *me*. This made him brave in my eyes. He was loving me despite the odds. People tried to break us up. There were lies told against me, and yet he stood by my side.

He knew I had a huge heart, loved people, and loved him. He said that he loved how I loved and took care of him. I catered to him, and I did so for many reasons; first, I enjoyed doing it; I wanted him to be happy. Secondly, to prove that I was really for him because he sometimes thought otherwise.

This was part of my identity issues. I even tattooed his name on my breast to prove my love and dedication to him. He did the same; his first and only tattoo is my name on his arm. We were seeking ways to prove our love to each other.

The first few years were explosive. After everything I've experienced in life, marriage is still the hardest I've tackled. But what makes it easier is the Lord at the helm, and my husband and I are committed to our marriage and our family. That commitment is everything because it holds us through the challenging times.

The Jig is up!

In the beginning, as I stated before, I was not very forthcoming about what I did for a living. "Office Manager," was the story I told everyone—even Frank. I kept this going for a long time—until we were invited to dinner at my best friend Malia's house, the one who started it all, the one whom I worked for. She was like family to me, as well as a friend. She would tell me not to share too much and never to volunteer information. I listened, but it blew up in my face.

Malia was a businesswoman who knew her stuff, and I had profound respect for her. She taught me the game. She was also my friend, and we spent time together regularly.

She invited Frank and me to dinner in her beautiful home in Beverly Hills, Michigan, where some of her neighbors were famous. We had a wonderful time.

After the dinner on the ride back home, I chatted and noticed Frank was silent. He broke his silence with a question: "So what does she really do?"

I was like, "She is a model." My usual response to that question. She certainly looked like one. She had some surgical enhancements that made you look as if she walked in any room. There was a certain "air" about her. When she talked about her life in conversations, it sounded fabulous and expensive. Heck, everything about her screamed money.

He said, "Bullshit," and proceeded to call me out on lies that he had been overlooking, and he said that he wanted to know the truth, all of it.

He wanted to know what type of stuff I was involved in, and he threatened to leave me if I wasn't completely honest.

Now by this time, he and I are very much in love, but you know that can turn sour quick with a bed of lies? Yeah, so take notes and *keep it real and honest if you want something real and honest*. Get it? I got it later.

Anyway, I told him *some* of the truth. Why? You would have to understand my life and mindset and how I had been truly living off-and-on since 17. I let him know that I was currently a scheduler—which I was—and that I was not presently doing sensual massages—which I wasn't.

I didn't admit that I had been an escort in the past—only to scheduling. I was scared and ashamed. I used to do all types of things before knowing him; that part wasn't a lie. I lied about how *deeply* I was involved in the past; some things just don't need to be said. I also lied about my bisexuality.

Bisexuality was another story altogether—but yes, that blew up in my face, as well. He was totally against it for his own personal reasons. He was adamant about this issue. He didn't like it point-blank, period. Divulging this information was unnecessary because it had nothing to do with him.

Today my husband and I have a great relationship. It's not without its struggles, but they are different struggles. We aren't the same people who got married in 2011; we have matured in our communication and acceptance of one another; Matured in the patience and grace we show each other—matured in how we love each other, even with how we disagree.

Change is inevitable; growth is not. Thankfully, I've matured. I am not the same woman he married. I am now saved and sanctified, and so much of what we did before doesn't go down today, yet we still enjoy each other's presence. I am no longer needy. I understand what I bring to this marriage and what he brings. I know who I am today, and that's different.

As a wife, I've learned to depend on him and respect him as my friend, husband, and the head of our household, and he has learned to trust me and allow me to "be." We can't change ourselves for other people. We can allow the Lord to change us, and He keeps the absolute best parts of us and uses it for His glory.

Now I answer Frank's questions without getting an attitude, and I've learned to ask a few myself. Balance, you know. (Wink) But we are still a work in progress. I know that God has given us grace for each other. There is much more I could type, but that would be another whole book.

OPPOSITES ATTRACT

We have learned many lessons in our journey, especially in blending our families, but for now, just know that we have learned that we don't own each other. We both belong to God, and our marriage is for His Glory.

I've learned to do all things to honor God and honoring my husband, marriage, and our family is honoring God. I matured in my marriage. I learned who I was in God and who He called me to be; trying to get there was a very tough road, and my marriage barely survived. I took my eyes from pointing out my husband's flaws and looked at myself.

The Lord forgave my past, which freed me, even if others wanted to bring it up. God forgave me, and I eventually forgave myself. When that happened, it was *nothing* anyone could say or do about my past that affected me. I was free!

I could tell it better and was willing to.

God accepted me! My thoughts were, *who are you*? That is why I can live my life authentically.

There is freedom in Jesus Christ!

JESUS STARTED CALLING ME

Neither Frank nor I went anywhere to worship, yet we were serious about our different beliefs. I still believed everything I was taught as a Jehovah's Witness, but because of my circumstances, as I previously shared, I chose to disassociate myself. Frank, likewise, believed in Jesus and used to be an avid churchgoer.

On July 4th, 2010, my beliefs would come into question—something I had never questioned in my life. This was a fork in the road experience, and it occurred at Frank's cousin's holiday barbecue.

That day his cousin called on everyone to join hands and pray before the food was served. It was a scene straight from a movie, and the day I heard the Lord for the first time.

I declined to hold hands and pray with them because, as a Jehovah's Witness (even an inactive one), I could not join hands in prayer with those who weren't in my religion. Everyone was standing, holding hands in a big circle in the backyard. There were benches there, and I was the lone woman sitting it out on the benches. Initially averting my eyes, I could feel the eyes staring at me. I looked bravely towards the group in a defiant way, feeling defensive.

Frank looked embarrassed, and on the ride home, questioned me about it. But see, my attitude was like, "Oh well" I mean, I was sorry he felt that way, but I thought that it was false religious worship, and I couldn't be a part of it. I stood firm in my beliefs, whether I was actively practicing it or not. He was mad at me.

Surprisingly in that same week, something started happening to me. I started hearing a voice and feeling like an impression inside of me that I needed to "dig deeper" into my religion and beliefs. I heard a voice speaking to me. *Is this God? Is this the voice Angela heard?* I wondered.

Again, I heard that voice say, "Dig deeper into your religion. Find the truth." I found myself talking to myself, saying, "No, I can't do that. That's apostasy." This was unfamiliar territory. I had feelings that were new and voices inside me that made me think I was crazy. I can't explain it, but it was like talking to myself, like my conscience speaking, saying, "Dig Deeper" and "Search out the truth." This occurred for several days.

At this point, the feeling was strong to dig deeper, and I couldn't shake it. I had to respond. It was scary because I knew it was "wrong" to do; however, I called Frank's sister and asked her to bring me a Bible. I had never read or studied anything other than the New World Translation in my life, yet something propelled me to search for answers. It was exhilarating and scary at the same time. She brought me a New International Version Bible and a study journal.

I started studying, reading line by line, comparing the different versions of the Bible, and looking up scriptures and the concordance on the internet.

"What is happening to me?" I would ask myself. It was all very strange and terrifying. It is important to realize that I was genuinely scared. If you've been in this situation, then you get it, but if not, then try to understand. I didn't know what was happening or why it was happening. I was doing things that I was told not to do the entire time I studied with the Witnesses. I felt crazy.

In any case, I did move forward. I kept digging and found that I didn't have to dig too deeply because there were tons of information to read on Jehovah's Witnesses and books written by ex-Jehovah's Witnesses. I even found websites dedicated to helping ex-Witnesses transition into normal society. Yes, it is that deeply ingrained in our brains that we need help knowing how to "live normally." I realized that I was worshipping an organization. They had put themselves equal to Jesus. They were the mediators between me and God the Father.

Thus, the research began! I started comparing Bible verses and versions. I love to research, so this was an enjoyable project. I still have those journals to this day. I was on the search for God; if Jehovah's Witnesses weren't "The Truth," then who or what was? I wanted God in my life, yet everything I knew was in question. How do I get to know God truly? Who was He? Were there three of them? More? Or only one? Was He the Universe? I had many questions, as my knowledge was expanded from the internet.

All my life, I tried; yet I was no closer to God than I had been when I was a child. What was I missing? I didn't want to be a heathen in the world, but that was my lot in life. I was a confused mess, wondering, "Can a Sista get some clarity?" I had a dream shortly after, which was the first of what would become many prophetic dreams for me. *I don't remember every aspect of my dream, but I do remember being in a field. I remember food sprouting up from the ground and on the trees, like vegetables and fruits. I was with someone but could not see their face clearly. I remember that the sky had scriptures written on it really huge; like everywhere you walked, you could see the scriptures. But I don't know which scriptures they were, exactly. Then, I started walking, and the next thing I knew, I was in a building, waiting to get inside. There was a long line, and everyone was going inside in pairs. So, I finally got in, and the room was filled with gold-and-diamond watches. No silver. I remember someone saying, "Real watches don't spin," or something along those lines, and the watch hands did not spin. There were also digital watches. Some were like gold keychain watches. I walked around the whole room, checking them out, and then decided that there were some watches I wanted to look over again. But they were gone. I started running around the room, looking for watches. Then, they began to disappear. There were only a few watches left when I woke up.*

When I woke up, the feeling that I got when the Word in the sky represented Jesus, and every eye would see Him. The second feeling was that He was coming soon, and time was running out. And the watch hands didn't turn and couldn't tell time because we don't know the exact time or hour, but we must keep on the watch. I praise God and thank God for this dream.

After that dream, I knew for sure that the Lord Jesus was trying to get my attention. It was a warning dream. I was excited but scared. After the July 4th incident, Frank and I made up and carried on with our relationship.

I remember praying to Jesus in my bedroom and being very afraid to do so after that dream. I was crying and saying, "Lord, I am scared. All my life, I was told not to pray to You, and yet here I am." I said I wanted to know who He truly was, that I wanted Him in my life. I acknowledged He died for me and rose three days later. I kept asking Jesus to save my life and show me the truth. The experience was extremely emotional. It was a huge turning point; at 33 years old, I had never gone directly to the Lord Jesus before and was scared. If you can imagine finding out everything you thought was the truth was a lie. Yes. That moment. It was deep.

What happened next was strange and wonderful. I felt warmth from the bottom of my feet to the top of my head, then it felt like a warm embrace. The atmosphere in my room shifted, and I felt love! My room was full of love! That is the best way to describe that feeling, like a hug from someone you love and who loves you. It was peaceful, and I smiled as my tears dried up. I knew in that moment Jesus met me where I was. I was forgiven! Right in my bedroom! To God, be the glory! It was such an exciting and beautiful moment. I laughed and felt a tremendous amount of joy. What in the world was happening? It was powerful, yet strange. I didn't believe in the supernatural, yet something supernatural was occurring.

I never had such a powerful experience before, and I was at home! I told Frank, and he was happy for me. After that day, I had an earnest desire to read the Word and know more. I even wanted to go to a church. Can you believe it? Me, at church? Now, *that* was a miracle. It would be about three years before I was baptized in Jesus' name and filled with the Holy Ghost with evidence of speaking in tongues.

God does know our hearts. Therefore, I know you can be in any religion, but if you desire him with a sincere heart, He will show Himself to you in a tangible way and bring you to Himself. He did it for me, and He is the same God. I was on a different road, but He called me and made Himself known to me.

If God changed me, He could change anyone, and I'm serious about that. In this way, I have compassion for others who are as blind as I once was. Some people just don't know. Heck, I didn't know.

Anyway, hence began my journey with the Lord.

THE NEXT DAY
~

Here is a journal entry that I wrote the next day of the incident at Frank's cousin's house, which started my journey to Jesus. I'm thankful that I've always journaled my thoughts since I was a teenager.

July 5, 2010, 10:44 AM

So, Frank was upset because I didn't hold hands during a prayer over the meal with his cousins and friends. I don't know if he remembers our arguments and conversations when he went to the memorial. He said he went "for me," which is great, but see; he had a huge issue about going. This was when we discussed not doing anything, we're not comfortable doing. I told him that I shouldn't be holding hands with everyone praying because I pray to Jehovah in Jesus's name. No prayer that I have seen was said to Jehovah. People pray to Jesus or to "Our Lord." See, during those same talks and fights, I said I wouldn't be doing it anymore because I did it at Christmas. It bothered me, made me uncomfortable. Last Christmas, while holding hands, I was talking and praying to Jehovah, saying, "I know this isn't pleasing to you, and I'm sorry." I have to take a stand in my life. I can't let others dictate what I do. They can't save my life. Yeah, I smoke. Yep. That's my weakness. I'm aware, and Jehovah's aware. I constantly pray about my smoking. He will help me if I try to help myself. But see, just because I smoke doesn't mean it's okay for me to do anything. Like I won't go worship in a church. No one's church. Only Kingdom Halls, where you learn about Jesus and Jehovah. I have to be me, and I serve Jehovah. I am a baptized servant. My life hasn't been the same since I was baptized into the Truth. I really want to get myself back in good standing before Jehovah cuts off the time. So, I'm more concerned with how Jehovah and Jesus view me than his cousins. Why can't I just be me? That's my question. I no longer want to "go along" just because everyone else is. And see, I knew this issue would come back up. It really only surfaces on holidays, holidays on which I can partake of food but not hold hands and join in a group prayer.

Here is a journal entry from the year 2000, when I was invited to a friend's church. I was excited when I found this entry. I had to include it.

December 17, 2000

C's church gives me the creeps. It's weird, and I don't want to go back. No. I'm not going back. I just have to figure out how to tell her. Spiritually, that church isn't good. What do you learn? They don't teach you how to walk in the way Jesus walked. The pastor is called a "prophet." And he makes them shake and shiver and babble in the so-called "Holy Ghost." They need to read the Bible more, and I feel terrible vibes when I'm there. That place is not for me. But she really won't understand—unless she really is my friend and respects my decision. If that is the case, then she will say okay, that's my decision, and she won't be mad.

This was after I came back from Baltimore. I rented an upstairs flat from my friend and her husband, and they invited me to church. I went out of curiosity, really, but when I arrived, I said Jehovah forgive me, and the church gave me the creeps. In hindsight, it wasn't because of anything they were doing. It was just a different belief system than mine, and as a Jehovah's Witness, I was self-righteous, and everything else was wrong if it wasn't a Witness. It was of the devil and would be destroyed, was my thinking.

THE NEXT DAY

When I read this and look back on different journal entries throughout the years, I laugh and shake my head. God has a sense of humor. He had mercy on me through all my decisions throughout my life, and now His grace sustains me. I didn't believe in speaking in tongues, and He has gifted me to speak regularly. It's amazing, really.

The relationship I now have with God is the best thing to ever happen to me. It's bigger than any church building. God opened my eyes to the religion I was in and called me to Himself. He met me in my bedroom! He could come anywhere at any time. Jesus is alive, and I learned that He would come if I asked Him into my heart and life. If I want to know Him, He will make Himself known. Yes, He called me—but I also *answered* the call. I didn't just let it ring and send Him to voicemail!

THE DEVIL'S MONEY

The escorting lifestyle initially seemed glamourous. I worked as an escort off and on for many years. All I had to do was look pretty and entertain men, and they would pay me. But of course, it was much more involved, like sex. Just like anyone else who works, you work for money, right? Well, this was no exception. I worked for money. It was good money too. I loved the trips and gifts, but after a while, it wasn't so glamourous. Yeah, it's cool when the guy is handsome with a toned body, which was good in bed, but you didn't always get that.

Sometimes it just felt dirty. You may think it's all dirty, and only someone who has experienced this knows what I mean. You could have fun times in this life, but other times feel degraded. On the one hand, lots of glamour, trips, gifts, and money. On the other, there was a physical danger that was present. Someone could hurt or kill you, and none would be the wiser. People already look down on prostitutes; who would care, right? (I say this line sarcastically)

Some men wanted so much for that money, more than you want to do. They think they own you because they are paying you. But I and other escort or providers had boundaries of what we would or would not do. It was posted in the advertisements and discussed. I tried to stick with those. It's like going to the grocery store hungry. You're likely to buy whatever, like lots of things you don't need. It may be a bad analogy but working when you need money and not just to keep stacking your money will make you cut corners. Even the best escorts have done it.

The sad part is I did things I said I would never do because the money was good. The *love* of money is a snare. I was paid thousands, not hundreds, for a particular session, but I felt like I sold my soul in that appointment. It was one of the catalysts for me wanting to leave the business. Never say what you will "never" do. Say, "I would hope I wouldn't do that." I used to say in the business, "I would never do that" to certain services, but that *right* circumstance came about, and I got high enough and said yes for a substantial amount of cash. Who had I become? You see, even reference checks don't always stop a crazy one from getting through. Providers booked this john because he was very generous. Although wealthy, he was into some sick stuff. That's all I will say about that.

Truly, I was risking my life every day I worked. Not only that but my sanity. Where was my self-respect? I went from feeling empowered to feeling debased. Not right away, but eventually, I walked away altogether and never sold my body again.

Fast forward to the fall of 2008; I was financially strapped. I knew I wouldn't sit in the rooms again, having sex with strangers, but I wouldn't mind scheduling others to do it. I contacted Malia to see what she had going on.

She had a position as manager of the commercial office studio located in Southfield, Michigan, and some other locations. Sex was prohibited in the office space; they had to take those clients to the apartment studio. Malia owned about four studios at the time. I was on the front line. She was the boss, and I was her manager. If the issue got to her, the girl was getting fired. She would tell me, "Don't bring anything to me unless I really need to know." I had to handle it. She paid me a salary—a generous one.

The office was on the basement floor in a professional building near Greenfield Rd and 10-mile Rd. I was there scheduling by phone, and email, taking the money, and making sure everything ran well. The girls would be booked back-to-back as they liked. The building was perfect because there were many businesses, and people were coming and going regularly.

There were two rooms in the suite. The guys came into the office, and I will be at the desk with the laptop. I would collect the money and call the girl out, and they would go into their session. Usually, the sessions were 1 hour in length at a minimum.

During this time in my life, it was a business. I worked as an escort and a sensual massage therapist, which helped me relate to the girls more.

The girls used to spin all kinds of stories, and I wanted to believe the good in them, and Malia would say, "T they lying" She didn't put anything past anyone.

As many as ten girls worked for us. The money was rolling in until it wasn't. You see, with working girls, when they made money, they disappeared until they needed money again; it was a problem. They felt like they were rich with a few thousands of dollars and gave me excuses for why they couldn't work.

We didn't want too big of a network because that may have attracted too much attention, so I was more careful with my scheduling. We found out that some of the girls had drug problems, and we wanted no part in that.

Sometimes, Malia would put ads in the newspaper seeking massage therapists, and either one of us would go and meet potential workers at a local restaurant for an interview after receiving a picture of them, a copy of their ID via email, and speaking by phone.

Usually, my approach was to introduce myself, and then I would ask them to sit down and chat with me for a bit. (I would already be at the restaurant) They would ask me where the massage therapy job was located, and I would ignore their question and instead ask something like, "What do you do now? Do you dance or anything?" Some of them would answer yes or say that they didn't currently dance, but they used to in the past.

I would then ask if they had ever given a sensual massage. Typically, they would say yes to this. Then, I would ask them if they were comfortable giving Malia or me a massage to see if they were qualified.

I would always ask if there was anything they wouldn't do and what was off-limits, so I would know what to schedule them for. And yadda-yadda-yadda.

This was a typical conversation, of course, not verbatim, and all of them ended up being escorts—even those who said they only wanted to do massage—because they realized the earning potential, just like I did when I transitioned from one to the other.

Women were a commodity. I was a commodity. There was no real care. It reminded me of what my old boyfriend said—and my thoughts were similar, "They are going to do it anyway. I might as well get their money."

Malia still worked as well and had her regulars. She didn't have to work, but she did when she wanted to. Most times, she had a sugar daddy taking care of her.

Anyway, when I was still an active escort, Malia and I both had gone to Chicago to work. The suburbs surrounding Chicago were a jackpot and a regular stop on our tour circuit. We met with some male friends who happened to be pimps for dinner and talked about the business. Believe it or not, it was an exciting life with some occasional downsides.

There were a lot of girls that started in the business as runaways in Chicago. Some said their parents put them out for one reason or another; being a lesbian, having a substance abuse problem, or being unruly and hardheaded, but they ended up on the streets of Chicago tricking. Many had been out there for years.

Some were in hotels; not all walked the streets. I was thinking about how the stories I heard were messed up. Many abused hard drugs. I saw girls who sold their bodies to afford their drug habit and used drugs to get through the various acts of prostitution.

Seeing what I saw; talking to the different pimps showed me another side to the business—a dark side. I didn't like that side. I wanted to go back to the pleasant hotel rooms and pretend that escorting was different; it was upscale.

BOSS LADY

In the latter part of 2009, Malia told me that the office and the girls weren't making enough to sustain all that she was putting in financially. (Note that when I say "girls," I am referring to the adult women who worked as escorts. We refer to them as "girls" in the business).

Malia said she was "shutting everything down," and I was like, "What am I going to do?" I was hurt and upset. The girls were upset and confused. There were a few who were loyal, but not all the girls were. Some were just a problem. Logically I understood, but I was in my feelings about her decision.

She and I got into an argument and didn't talk for a while. Falling out with Malia to this magnitude was a first for us, and we both said hurtful things. It was a sad time for me because Malia was like family to me and a close friend and confidant. We later reconciled, but I was doing my own thing at this time, and she did hers.

Two of the girls asked if they could still work for me when the office closed; I said, "Sure," because I needed money also. They were both pretty Caucasian women with long blonde hair and big breast, which in this business equaled money.

They were popular, and I knew I would do well with them and make good money. Immediately, I set up ads online and in the paper for them, and the phones were ringing off the hook. Time was money.

I could have had more girls, but after seeing the issues Malia faced, I decided against it. I did well with them, and everything was running smoothly.

I started working on those phones and scheduling the girls with their dates during in-calls at hotels. I didn't schedule any outcalls. At this point, I wasn't trying to be straight and fly right, I was about to do my own thing, and I was excited with the monetary possibilities.

I enjoyed this when everything was going smoothly. I recruited one Black girl, and she worked at the Eastside hotels. I took photos of her and placed her on the internet, as the other girls were; the other two were in Southfield. Each day, I would drive to meet them at the end of their shift and get my money. It was a great arrangement.

One of the girls started acting up not too long after working for me, and I had to get verbally aggressive with her. Another time, I didn't send her many clients, and she would call me asking if it's slow. She came around, and we were able to get back to focusing on getting money. But after about a year, I ended up firing her; her coke habit trumped her work ethic. She had started getting complaints and bad reviews, that's a no-no; it kills a business.

Multiple phones and a laptop were on me everywhere I went. It wasn't easy to maneuver during hair school because I had to find a spot to talk discreetly. I kept the phones on vibrate.

"Why do you have so many phones?" Someone asked at school

(I was asked on more occasions than I can count.) I smiled, "I like phones." I was sarcastic.

I would sometimes ignore the question altogether, looking right at them. *None of your business,* I would think (and sometimes, say out loud). I was not always the nicest person all the time—especially when I felt checked. I had a lot to hide, so I didn't want people too close to me. *I don't ask people questions; why are they intent on asking me questions?* I would think.

I didn't have a studio at this time; I had a hotel with a hookup, and my girls could rent two rooms monthly.

Other girls were working there. Many hotels are full of escorts. Some have the pimp in a room, and they would be in several different rooms working. I would go to the hotel now and then and sit in the parking lot and watch the traffic. I would move my girls if I thought it was too hot. I could always spot a john and a working girl. *How?* I couldn't explain it to you, but I know that I see them out even today. There is a look.

My "Megan" voice was a high-pitched, valley girl, but professional voice.

Ring

"Hello, this is Megan".

"Hello Megan, this is Tom. I was responding to your ad on Escort

Vault for Natalie."

"Hi Tom, great, she would love to see you; what references would you like me to check on your behalf?"

"I've seen Jan and Susie."

"Okay, give me your contact info and any information that will help them remember you, and I'll call you back with an answer."

At this point, I would call both providers and check their references. Many times, if I didn't know the providers, I would look them up and see how long they had been working and if they had any references on the various sites. But I still needed to speak to them by phone or email.

Once all was checked out, I would call and confirm a schedule with the john.

The price point was different for different girls based on their looks and reviews. Regular updated photos were a must. Also, we encouraged reviews. As with any service, they help to get more clientele. This business was running like a legitimate business.

Some johns gave up their work information to confirm who they were. I would then call and ask for them after checking the website and any information about the company.

Of course, if a sting operation were in play, all that would be fabricated. I thank God that I was never involved in a sting, but I was aware when they went down because we would tighten up and only see regulars.

With my own business, I met the girls daily and picked up my money. We only met at the same spot a few times. We had to keep switching it up as to not bring attention to ourselves.

Of course, some gave their numbers to the guys directly and cut out the middleman. I know because they stop calling me to book. I'm not crazy. I had books, and I knew all the clients' names and numbers.

I had different phone numbers, and some would try to call the other lines, pretending to be someone else, and I would burst their bubble quickly. I had been in the business in one form or another for over ten years.

The girls still needed me to schedule because the bulk of their income came through me, and vice versa. If they didn't work, I didn't get paid. I wanted to keep a low profile, so I didn't expand beyond the three girls. They also preferred not to talk to the clients on the phone; they just wanted to do the work.

I never broke character with the girls. They knew me as Megan. I wasn't their friend. If I were extra friendly, boundaries could easily be crossed, and respect could be lost. I've seen it happen.

Listen, I was not trying to stop what I was doing. It was great money, and I wasn't hurting anyone. People say prostitutes break up families. I beg to differ. The person who *decides* to step out on their spouse is breaking up the family. Whether a prostitute or just a regular girl, there is always someone willing to be that other woman. Except in the case of a prostitute, they are getting paid to be whatever the man or john needs them to be for a specified period. If the man is looking to step out, he will. People do what they want. They look for trouble, and they find it. The desire they have inside will manifest to action, and because this world is full of all types of evil, it's easy to find. We are a fallen world with fallen natures.

My mind is made over, and I wouldn't do those things today or want my children doing them, but I understand what it's about because I did live that life. It's a life of pretense.

That life gave me financial freedom—even though I spent money as fast as I got it on whatever I wanted, or my children wanted. Unfortunately, I didn't know how to be a good steward of my money. There was the god of my belly that I bowed down to, metaphorically speaking. We ate well daily. My children didn't eat hot dogs and chicken legs, etc. (just an example), but steaks and lobsters. Let me digress for a moment and tell you something that made me laugh. When Frank and I got together, he was so shocked that my children ate what I ate. I thought that was hilarious. But I wanted them to have a diverse palette, not just eating chicken every day. His palette changed being with me also.

I was a giver, so I would pay for drinks and dinners for whoever was there. I paid the tab. When I went out with Malia, she did that for her friends and family, and that's something I picked up from her. She is a giver. People who were around me knew that I had them. It was understood. I would help with a bill or whatever. I got you if you let me know—I mean, I'm not a mind reader. Ha, ha!

So, you must understand that when my friend Angela came calling, saying I had to give up my business, I couldn't feel that. Who was I without my alter-ego, Megan? I had been Megan for the past ten years secretly. I started as Cherry Red, the dancer, and she evolved into Megan Simone, Escort, and Madam. Some knew; some didn't. I liked Megan. And now, Angela said that I should walk away because it was the "Devil's money." I was being blessed. That's how I looked at it.

It was the spring of 2011. I was about to get married next month. I had just graduated from hair school. Angela called me and told me the Lord said that I must stop taking the devil's money.

She was so adamant, so serious! She had told me the same thing the year before, right before I moved out of my townhouse where I was her neighbor.

That first time I hadn't heard any words from the Lord and didn't understand how she knew what the Lord wanted. I didn't believe prophets still existed. She talked strangely sometimes, but I liked her.

At the end of the day, *I wasn't ready to give up the money.* The crazy thing is she didn't know what I was doing. She said that the Lord started revealing it to her when He gave her the Word for me.

I had been her neighbor for about two years. I told her I was an office manager, just like I told many people. So, her coming and telling me what she knew blew my mind. *What's this? Some type of witchcraft?* I wondered.

This time, Angela said that the Lord wanted to bless me, and I had to step out on faith because He had things in store for me, a path that He'd set, but I had to let this go first. I was moved to tears this time around because I was able to receive this word now. I believe it was because of my experiences with the Lord calling me Himself after that incident at Frank's cousin's barbecue.

"What will I do? How can I trust God will take care of me?" I asked. See, I trusted in the money I was making. I trusted that every day that phone would ring, and I would have money to pick up.

It was money that was consistent. Everything was going so well, until she called, saying that I had to give it up. That was incredibly hard; it hurt. I didn't know how to truly trust God—even after my bedroom experience in 2010.

Walking by faith in God was a foreign concept to me. I walked by faith in my money, and faith in my business, faith in myself, but to me, that was tangible. I couldn't know for sure that God would take care of me. It was my choice, of course. God didn't strong-arm me.

A week or two later, I talked to the girls to let them know I was leaving the business, and my top girl Angie and I agreed on an amount, and I sold the phone to her. Yes, I sold it; it was full of names, numbers, and info. It was my little black book; I wasn't going to give it away.

I discussed this with Frank before making these moves. He was like, *what are you going to do*? I hadn't filled out a job application or interviewed in God only knows how long. I had been scheduling girls our entire relationship, and the money I brought in daily was great. He made good money as well, and so our situation was ideal.

There was a brief period that he was laid off and received unemployment; 6/7 months, and I was able to take that slack up. We all depended on that money. Not solely, but it was a factor. Many times, we lived recklessly and for the moment. I had always lived that way. It was time to grow up and be responsible.

He was getting used to the lifestyle with me, so this was about to be a huge change. But I knew in my heart that it was time. Besides, I had started to become paranoid in the business.

When Frank went back to work, I was out of work for the first time since I was 14 years old.

What now?

NEW PLACES, NEW FACES

❧

After months of studying after my bedroom experience, I talked with my husband, and we agreed it was time to visit a church. My family and I attended two churches on-and-off: one nondenominational church with my friend Angela; and a Baptist church with my cousin.

They were vastly different; the Baptist church was large, and the other was small; one was more conservative in their preaching style, and the other was more dramatic. They both taught a triune God, which was very new to me, so I started researching the term "The Trinity." I saw that the churches didn't agree if there was or was not a trinity.

In the nondenominational church, both the husband and wife preached. They were pastor and co-pastor. I had never seen a woman teaching or preaching from the pulpit before. In the Hall, we had theocratic ministry school, and the women could give demonstrations on how to conduct a Bible study or what to say when out in service, but the men taught. This was all so interesting, and I watched it like it was a good television show. I felt like a tourist!

The husband was a prophet, or so they said, and he gave predictions to many in the congregation each time we attended. I didn't believe in prophets for today, so I didn't know how to feel about the things the pastor said; however, I was interested in gathering information and watched everyone with curiosity. I became absorbed with church life and the people.

Despite totally disassociating myself from the Witness religion, I found myself comparing many doctrinal beliefs. It was difficult and took time to unlearn what I believed for so long.

As I continued visiting churches, I became confused by the different doctrines taught at various churches and knew that was not the way it should be.

In the Bible, groups that taught different beliefs were called sects; they broke off from "The Way" (the true followers of Jesus). I looked at all these churches as sects. I didn't know what to believe or where to go. I started watching different ministers on television like Joyce Meyer, T.D. Jakes, Joseph Prince, and Creflo Dollar.

Although I had that amazing experience in my bedroom, I still had questions and didn't understand God's supernatural aspect. I needed to understand logically.

For this reason, when I saw people doing odd things, like speaking in tongues and receiving prophecies, I felt like it was not the right church for me; however, I was quite fascinated by it all.

I didn't realize it at the time, but every church atmosphere I experienced was necessary for my learning. God showed me how different people worship Him to allow me to get comfortable with the diversity amongst believers; we are all one body that has many parts.

No one denomination has all the answers. Everyone wants to be right. We box Him in, but He is BIGGER and far GREATER than we could even imagine.

Frank and I weren't fully committed to the church life. We still drank, partied, and did everything we wanted to do. We visited churches off-and-on with no real dedication. Our understanding was that God knew our hearts, which made things okay for us.

I struggled with a vicious cycle of going back and forth; I always felt a pull to come to God, but I would quit, then start again. Inside of me, something new was happening. I was feeling conviction where I didn't before; at least, not so heavy.

I wanted to fully give my life to God and live right, but the world and its vices were also pulling at me.

Smoking weed was my problem more than drinking; it was a bad habit that I enjoyed. I wasn't begging God to take it away.

Anyway, at one of the churches we attended, the pastor had a prophetic word and would call on people during service. One Sunday, as we were leaving, the Pastor was at the door, saying goodbye to everyone as they went. As I walked past, I said, "See you at bible study, Pastor." His response was "new places, new faces." I was confused. But I would later understand that I was being moved; that wasn't my church home. That was my last Sunday.

I wanted to learn about the church, and I was hungry for the Lord at the time. Hungry for some truth.

As a result, I did what I normally did as a Witness; when I was in it, I was in it to the fullest! In church, I found myself doing the same. There is nothing wrong with committing.

During my second year of marriage, I worked as a salon supervisor in Eastpointe when I met a new client, who propelled me even further in my walk.

It was one of those divine connections that I've had throughout my journey. She invited me to her church, and I had a wonderful experience.

The pastor's words spoke to me somewhere deep as if no one else was in the room. I felt that was where I was supposed to be. I was excited. This was the "new places, new faces" phrase being manifested in my life. I answered the altar call and joined the church.

My husband was disappointed that I joined a church without him, as we were supposed to find a church home together. He was working on that Sunday when she invited me, and I went anyway to check it out. I didn't intend on joining.

Another time, he didn't want to go, so the girls and I attended church alone. That became the routine; me asking if he wanted to go, and him saying no. However, he would come from time to time and tell me everything that was wrong with the church, the pastor, and the members.

What I learned afterward is that I started it all wrong. I was out of order with many things, out of biblical order. But I was still very headstrong and willful.

I changed a lot during this time for the better. At times, I was a bit self-righteous—new Christian and all; you know how it is. It was no accident that I met her on that day. It was a divine connection. God was intervening and putting me back on the path.

I stopped smoking again after a long off-and-on struggle with marijuana. I was there for quite some time. I learned about church culture there. I worked in the ministry and loved it. I used my talents in the church for God's glory. He gifted me with it. I was able to do things with technology that no one taught me. That's a gift.

It wasn't all bad. There was a purpose for me to be there during that time. I learned how to worship at that church and say, "Hallelujah! Praise God! And thank You, Jesus!" out loud with confidence and to go boldly to the throne of grace! Also, I learned how to do church announcements and media slides. I became close to the pastor's administrative team, and I started helping in many ways. I enjoyed it. Gifts were being stirred in me; some, I didn't even know were there. They taught me that the many gifts I used in the world would be used by the Lord for His glory. I also learned how to make the best sweet potatoes ever! There was always a lot of cooking each Sunday.

I was often trying to get my husband to attend regularly with the girls and me. He said that something was rubbing him the wrong way there, and he didn't like how they looked at him and talked to him. I would later learn that a few would accost him when I wasn't around saying words to him, such as, he wasn't saved, and he was under my covering until he was saved.

The church was strict, yet I didn't mind the militant and legalistic way it was run because coming from Jehovah's Witness, I was used to strictness. The downer for me is that I was attending church feeling like I had to choose between my husband and the church, based on the information I was being told.

At this point, all hell was breaking loose in my home. I still didn't leave the church.

I am not naming the church or its members because it's not about them. It's about my experiences there and how all this shaped me on my journey. God was still in this. What truly hurt me is the friends that I thought I made for life, the sisterhood. It all came to an end when I left the church. That felt like what Jehovah's Witnesses do to those who leave their Organization.

My husband wanted me to leave. I remember one day, crying as I left church. We were all prepping and preparing for some event. Some of the sisters were just so mean and spoke to me any kind of way. Me and my oldest, Tyler, were not in the same section but ended up both being hurt by different people that day and crying about it.

My husband was like, "Don't go back there. Let's find a church together." I was still on the fence because I didn't know how to leave. It's like I was in bondage all over again. During this time, the Lord moved me from the Eastpointe salon to a new salon in Oak Park in December 2012.

Everywhere I'd been since letting the phone and that lifestyle go was divinely orchestrated. No one can tell me different. God was setting my path straight. Regardless of the trials, I saw His unchanging Hand.

Fast-forward to the beginning of spring 2013, and I am in Oak Park, working in my own salon suite. It was my first private suite. I was usually on the open floor with the other stylists. This was nice and personal, and I could control the atmosphere, the music, and so forth. Let me show you how God moved in my life to shift me. He does it in your life also. You must pay attention because He does weave Himself into situations to work them out for our good.

On a Tuesday, the owner Kim came in, and she was never there on a Tuesday. Kim was a minister who operated in the prophetic. (Do you notice how I keep being around prophetic people)? She came to my room and said that she was specifically looking for me because she had a Word for me, but she didn't know what it meant, and that God wanted me to search it out and seek Him for understanding. The Word was, "Don't kick the pricks."

I was like, "Uh, what?"

She told me that He laid that on her heart to say to me.

After much research and prayer, I understood. I was going against what God was trying to do and what He was speaking through my husband.

It was time for me to leave the church. I couldn't let my marriage fall apart over a church building, a pastor, or a congregation.

Even after all this, for a newly acclimated girl to church life, it didn't deter me. I thank God that I pressed on and didn't give up on Him or His people, as many do who've shared similar situations.

WHAT HAVE I GOTTEN MYSELF INTO?

Man, this is crazy, I thought. *How do I leave sure money, and now, I'm trying to figure out how we will pay these bills? There is still so much to do with the wedding; why couldn't God ask me to give up the phone after my wedding? And after we were settled in as husband and wife? Jeez, this is tough.* I was in my head, but I couldn't articulate my thoughts to my new husband. We didn't even understand what a rude awakening this was about to be.

My wedding was amazing! One of the best days of my life.

Suddenly, our financial reality set in shortly after. I didn't have a job and had just graduated from hair school; normally, I would either go into the business myself or get some girls to work for me, but those days were over. That life was over.

I remember my friend Wanda, whom I met at the new church we were attending, told me that the Lord told her, "The life you live, you live no more," when He called her from darkness to Light. He didn't say those exact words to me, but He was calling me to His Light, and the meaning was the same.

The process had already begun. I had to trust God. I vowed to trust *Him*. He said that He had me, so I decided to see what He was about to do. What did His "having" me look like? I wasn't going to do my normal thing. I would push through because I wanted to see what Jesus was going to do. *How was He different? What was He going to add to my life?* I put Him to the test.

I soon discovered that He started taking things, not material things, (well that changed too) but stuff from inside me. The parts that needed to go. He took my hurt and insecurity. He helped me love myself.

The other part—changing into a regular person—was another thing altogether. So, for me, this was tough. God wanted me to depend on Him and my husband. I always took care of myself. I didn't answer to anyone. Yes, I know I was married before, but he and I would take care of things together financially, and that whole situation was simply different.

This new marriage was nothing like any relationship that I'd ever had because my husband held me accountable for what I did and the words I said. He didn't want to argue—let alone fight. He would constantly say, "Tara, I'm not your enemy."

Yea, well, it seems like it was my response.

We went through trials and tribulations as with any new marriage. We had a blended family with his son and my two daughters. It was perfect! Or so I initially thought. You see, I always wanted a son, but at that time, my new son didn't quite want me. I didn't know what to do with that. He already had a mom, but not two sisters, so he gained the sisters with our union, and he adored them. I was sort of just there.

My youngest daughter didn't quite want Frank. Tyler was

neutral. This presented a new set of issues that we didn't expect. We had to learn to co-exist lovingly. Blending families can be difficult, and ours was no exception.

That first year was rough financially because there were so many changes with my husband and me. I had to learn to work a regular job again, getting regular pay, and it had been several years for me. Ordinary people and regular pay sucked.

That year the Lord truly humbled me and showed me that He alone was my provider. And it hurt! That year we experienced utility shut offs. My children were like, *what is going on*. It was a first for them. Through all of that, everything was paid, and everything worked out. We were not put out of our home even though we were late with our rent for a straight year.

I had thoughts of going back to the business. I thought *I could make this money quick and jump back out*. But I determined to stay the course. It was tough!! Frank and I were bickering about everything.

At this time, I had graduated f r o m hair school and started working in a hair salon in Centerline, MI. From there, I started my hair career. I've had so much success in my professional career as a hairstylist in such a brief time. It was definitely God.

He was showing me that I could trust Him and that He would take care of me. Every salon I went to was better than the last, and everywhere I went, I prospered. I was even promoted to the salon manager several times. I never fell back. My clients, skills, and money grew. It felt good to make an honest, legal living. It was good money, too. My new issue to tackle was time management.

As I progressed in the industry, and my clientele rose, I began to work so much that I left home early and returned late, especially as a Salon manager and stylist. That was a busy job. Early mornings and late nights; that was my life. When my husband would say something, I would get angry because it wasn't like I was in the streets; I was working and making money.

At the time, I didn't understand that he just wanted to spend more time with me; so did my children. Frank didn't articulate it well. When he brought it to me, he was already frustrated. Then I became frustrated. I was very defensive; I can admit that now. Especially when I felt I was right.

It would have been awesome if my husband and I were all on the same page at the same time. I got saved within our marriage, and that made for more conflict. I was changing, and my husband wasn't altogether pleased. He didn't marry the *new* me; so, there were a lot of adjustments taking place.

There were times when I felt pressure to drink with him because he was drinking. I didn't like the "Oh, you don't drink anymore," "Oh, you don't smoke anymore," comments. I wasn't strong enough yet to say, "No, I don't," and leave it alone. I was fighting against my flesh. Who knew that after being baptized, I would go through that?

Our circle hadn't changed, so everything was still going the same way; *I* was just changing. That is an awkward place to be in. If you've experienced this, then you know what I mean. You want to be on one accord with your husband, but if he isn't connected with God, it causes problems. This takes strength in the Lord and having no fear of man. If we are honest, we can admit to having a fear of man. The Lord didn't put it in the Bible for nothing.

Frank and I had a tumultuous year that could have broken us and almost did. Without God, it would have. We split up for the first time.

I left and took my children to my cousin's house, where we stayed the night, and then I got a room where we could stay. I had never left my husband before. That was the first time and I'd involved my children. I knew it was over.

I remember travailing on my knees, saying, "God, I can't do this anymore. You have to do something. I can't; I am tired. I am done." I cried to God, "If you want this, then do something!" I felt defeated. There was no fight left. Have you ever felt that way? Like you've done all you could, and you just want to walk away?

I left in anger, not intending on returning, coming to grips with my marriage being over.

But God used my good friend Wanda, Angela, and my mother-in-law to mend my family. He worked through them in words they spoke to us and worked through us with a receiving heart.

The words that were spoken through them broke our hearts' fallow ground, and we worked it out. Soon after, the Lord blessed us with the purchase of our new home. He was moving us into a new season. A new chapter—it was time.

We needed a fresh start.

I thank God for not putting more on us than we could handle and making the way out. He mended my marriage.

A Word from the Lord December 27, 2015, that I wrote in my journal:

Today, God said to walk by faith and not sight. He said that everything I touch will be blessed. He said to stay the course and continue to be obedient. He said that He brought me back to Him when I stayed away. He said it's He who keeps my husband and me together. He said that He knows how to bring Him in and to remove my hands from Him. Trust Him. He says that He will give me the words to say because I don't know what to say, that He will put His words in my mouth. He says to write down what He shows me, and He will give me meaning, by and by. He says that I can't know everything right away. He says that He is doing a miraculous thing in my household and in my family. End of word

Glory to God!

God has taught me who He was in my marriage with Frank. He showed me the right and wrong ways to live and love. I learned how to have healthy expectations, and it took me to another level. It was extremely painful to learn these lessons because they affected my marriage, but they were necessary. Today, I know how to correctly love my husband and my children— and best of all, I love me!

PMDD

For the bulk of my life, I had a condition that went undiagnosed. It reared its ugly head in my marriage, and my husband was at the end of his rope; my children were tiptoeing around me, and I finally made an appointment to see my doctor after I went into another rage.

This time, I destroyed many wedding pictures and frames by throwing everything, and we were in our 2nd year of marriage.

Even though I leveled out after about a week, each week, every month was wreaking havoc on my marriage, not to mention my mindset and peace.

I had episodes throughout our relationship before getting married, but I was so high that the weed mellowed me out. That's one of the reasons he liked me to smoke, but I understood. I liked the relaxed weightless feeling the marijuana high gave me.

During my appointment with my primary care provider, I explained what I had been going through for most of my adult life. She told me it sounded like PMDD, which was an acronym for "premenstrual dysphoric disorder." I suffered from anxiety, depression, and anger for many years, always before my menstruation.

She said that many doctors didn't know about it because it was new on the scene and they were still incorrectly diagnosing women with PMS. They used to just say "PMS" but discovered that women were behaving erratically and having bouts of depression about 7-10 days before the first day of their period, and it was more intense than just PMS.

I fell into the PMDD category. My doctor suggested therapy before medication and referred me to Dr. Matthews. I quickly made an appointment. At this point, I was like, "Something gotta be done."

I arrived and was ushered into a small, dimly lit room with a desk, two chairs, a couch, and some plants. I looked around, thinking that it reminded me of a movie scene, but I couldn't quite place the movie.

I was nervous and apprehensive about seeing her. Therapy didn't have a good rep in my community. But as I stated before, it was time.

Dr. Matthews gave me a welcoming smile and invited me to sit in a chair or on the couch, whichever made me comfortable, she said. I chose the couch. I had lots of issues; this wasn't a chair conversation.

For a few seconds, I sat and watched her watching me. She was an older white woman, with wrinkles under her eyes, black and gray hair pulled back in a bun, small stature with slacks and a sweater. She had a notepad and pen, and I was sitting across from her, wondering if and how she could help me? How could she even relate to me?

Quickly I began to realize, after the first visit, that she helped me quite a bit. She asked the right questions, and she had such an air about her that made me feel comfortable sharing.

I realized through therapy that I had been walking around depressed and insecure for most of my life. I knew about the behavior around my "time of the month." But after going deeper, revisiting certain experiences and situations, I discovered how my past was influencing my present state. I had never dealt with any of the issues that happened in my life. I didn't know how; I would put it out of my head and continue with my life, but what was happening was a buildup of anger that would come out when triggered.

My defenses and anger would surface with my husband because he had an amazing way of patronizing me while speaking in a calm voice, and when I was aggravated, I would yell or throw things. He would then look at me, saying, "See, I knew it would come, you always do this..." and tell me I was the problem. I was *always* the problem when there was a problem, and I couldn't take it. I would lose control and become combative. It wasn't fair to me! He wasn't perfect!

I spoke to her about these things, and she gave me techniques to recognize my triggers and practice keeping my temper in check. I realized while in therapy that I didn't spend enough time with myself. I had no clue who I was or what I wanted. I went from man to man, man to woman, woman to woman throughout my life thus far. It was an unhealthy pattern. Also, I had walls up in my relationships (friendships, family, and marital relationships) that would take time to break down, brick upon brick. Still, if I was consistent and committed to being better, then I would get there.

I had to take control of myself. I needed to get my voice back; it was stolen from me. *Who was I? Why was I who people wanted me to be, even in my marriage? What did I genuinely want?*

Dr. Matthews said I could create the life I wanted, but it would take me being honest with myself and standing up for myself, but not with violence, with words. I realized how defensive I'd been with people and distrusting. It's just that I'd seen so much in my lie; it made my viewpoint jaded. I also realized that I deserve to be respected and loved, not just for what I could do sexually. Also, to stop making excuses for bad behavior in other people. That needed to change. But all of this was a process.

Therapy may be frowned upon in the Black community, but I am an advocate for it. Dr. Matthews tremendously helped me. She was great. It was emotional and difficult, but I had to face my hurts and expose my wounds.

However, therapy alone didn't help my PMDD, and I was prescribed Zoloft. I took that for several months, until one day, I didn't need it anymore. I can't explain it except to say the Lord delivered me. I didn't do it, nor did the medication. I didn't even take it a year. One day I woke up and didn't take it, then the next, and so on. The episodes never returned. Glory to God!

Zoloft doesn't heal PMDD. Just like most medications, it helped my symptoms. But it also made me like a zombie. I went from having too much emotion to having none. But again, you do what you need to do. I had to take it for a while. God gave us doctors. Use them.

SAVED AND SMOKING

I joined my current church towards the end of the summer in the year 2013. I attended my first women's weekend ever and met new church friends; several months later of the same year, I was baptized in Jesus name, and the following month filled with the Holy Spirit with the evidence of speaking in tongues. The Lord was moving quickly.

I was amazed to be speaking in another language. The day I received that gift, I was surrounded by bright light and a feeling of love. The light seemed iridescent— it was beautiful. I knew I was again in the presence of God like in my bedroom, but this was an even greater experience. I was in awe, and I kept making a sound like a sigh of contentment with a smile that seemed to be stuck in place.

Unspeakable joy followed.

So, after all of that, how did I end up saved and smoking? Keep reading…

In March of 2015, I had carpal tunnel surgery. I worked hard and enjoyed what I did, so having to sit down for six weeks and not do hair was terrible.

Not to mention, I had the wrong attitude about it and was angry. *How would I make money?* I didn't want to depend on my husband. I never wanted anyone holding anything over my head in what they did for me—Even him. I had a tantrum. Irrational fear set in; *I couldn't depend on him.* That was far from the truth, but I wasn't thinking straight.

Why was life so hard now?

Just a few weeks before my surgery, the Lord had opened yet another door, and I was in a great personal salon suite in Birmingham, MI.

I was ready to work! I loved doing hair and was a bit depressed about not contributing financially or driving my vehicle, and I had no clue how to rest. I was at the mercy of others and needed help for everything. This made me uncomfortable.

During this time, I applied and received a medical marijuana card. Yes, I hadn't smoked in a while, but I was in pain, mentally and physically, and wanted relief.

A door was opened that made it easy to get, and my injury was the ticket. And I wanted to smoke. It was a rough time emotionally in my life and marriage; I needed an escape.

Let me digress for a moment. I want to talk about temptation after being baptized, and even Holy Ghost filled with the evidence of speaking in tongues. I recall not smoking and thinking I was strong enough to be around it. God delivered me, and I was good, but I went out of town to visit a cousin of mine, and everyone was smoking weed. I didn't smoke the first two days, but by that 3rd day, I hit that blunt and returned to smoking again like it never left me.

SAVED AND SMOKING

It just showed me that it's more than saying you're delivered. It's acting in accordance with that deliverance. It's not allowing yourself to be in situations that could tempt you. We are tempted by what's in us. What draws me may not necessarily tempt you. I wasn't strong enough to be around it.

When I smoked weed with my new legal, medical card, my smoking was the worst—not to mention my PMDD was in overdrive. See, there is so much that I was experiencing. PMDD was the root of many of my issues—at least, that is what I thought at the time. I thought I could dabble in and out that I could play the devil's game, but he would show me.

I felt good because I had a legal card. I justified it by saying that I was following the law of the land. I would go to the dispensaries and regularly smoke. I had it under control.

My house was peaceful again.

All was well. Frank liked it when I smoked; he told me so. I wasn't yelling and acting nuts during my PMDD episodes; it kept me chill.

During this time, I was still attending church and working in the ministry. I recall one Tuesday, at our new church, the Bishop was teaching at Bible study, and he mentioned the legal marijuana cards, and that they don't give us an excuse to smoke, and so forth.

He wanted us to sign something or another regarding the city of Warren and the dispensaries. I didn't sign it because I had a card and didn't want to be exposed.

I promise you that the Holy Spirit was speaking to me that day. Now, I felt convicted when I went to the dispensary. I started looking around to see if anyone saw me. I didn't do that before; I walked with my head high, not caring who saw me. I was sick and needed my medicine. My attitude was: *What's the problem?*

At home, I would light lots of incense and smoke in my room or the bathroom. I enjoyed smoking weed. The funny thing is, I don't light incense today, but I did every time I smoked weed.

I also would go hide in the garage. But when I did, one of the kids would be looking for me. It never failed. I would sneak and hide somewhere, they would catch me, and I would yell at them for exposing me. It was irritating because I was trying to hide.

I tried not to smoke in the house, but sometimes I was too lazy to go outside. I loved to smoke in the bathroom, so I'd wet a large towel and put it at the bottom of my bathroom door to capture the smoke while burning an incense with the window cracked—the same for the bedroom.

My children would look sideways at me, so I explained to them that it was legal, and it was my medicine.

One day, my youngest daughter Devin (who was 10 or 11 at the time) said to me, "Mom, if that weed is for your medicine, then why do you do it with other people? Why do you party and do your medicine?"

Oh, wow, more conviction. My baby girl was sincere, but I felt checked. She was right, of course. Devin is wise and outspoken. I encouraged my children to have a voice. I talked to them, and I listened. She knew it wasn't right and called me out on it. She would start by saying something like, "Mommy, I'm not trying to be rude or mean, but can I say something?" Ha, ha! Yes, that's my Devin.

In April, two weeks post-surgery, Wanda invited me to a Sunday morning prayer at another church. It started early, at 6 am. I wasn't too thrilled about the time, but she said it blessed her and would bless me.

I remember it well.

As we pulled up and parked the car, I saw a small, unassuming church in the middle of a residential neighborhood with homes to the right and left of it. We got out of her van, and as we walked in, I noticed it felt different. I can only explain it as an electrical charge in the air, and the closer I got to the altar, the stronger it was.

We walked up the stairs, with Wanda leading the way, and as I entered the sanctuary, a Black older woman was wearing all white; a white headscarf and a white dress that reached the floor. She looked intently at me without breaking her prayer.

I looked around, noticing that it wasn't crowded. About twenty people were praying in tongues; some were doing it quietly, with their heads bowed. I sat in the third row from the front, at the end of the pew, discreetly looking around before I bowed my head to pray.

The lady in all white was Mother Johnson, and after she prayed, she started calling certain people to come stand before her for a personal prayer and a Word from the Lord. She looked at me with eyes that seemed as though she could see straight through me and motioned for me to come up.

I had a heavy heart that morning, contemplating separating from my husband because things were so strained with us. We had an issue that occurred that, for some reason, we couldn't get past. It was lots of resentment and the blame game, and we weren't vibing. Every little thing turned into an argument.

As I stood before her with my arms outstretched towards Heaven, timid but also excited for what the Lord had to say, she poured oil over my head and started talking to me with her piercing brown eyes looking directly into mine.

She said that God had opened a door for me, and my new job would be better than my last. (At the time, I was about to go to a new salon, so that was on point). She said that I had the power to take down the strongholds in my household and that God had already equipped me. She continued, saying, I had to keep looking to Him and trusting Him.

All of that was all good, but then she said something that stopped me in my tracks; "You have the power to break that stronghold. You gotta stop what you're doing. I'm not going to say it out loud because you know what I'm talking about. But you gotta stop that now. That's a stronghold, and other things will move when you break it."

I knew at once it was the weed, but I didn't want to hear that. I wanted to hear something about my marriage. She said everything would start working itself out after that. I couldn't continue in that manner. God had something better for me. A better life.

I didn't think smoking was the problem. I didn't see that there were demonic strongholds in my household that I had the power through Jesus to break. I didn't know I had any power. I was waiting on the Lord to miraculously heal my land. But I hadn't turned my face towards him and repented of what I was doing.

I was permitting the strongholds to be there with the choices that I was making. God was speaking a word through her, but it didn't look like what I thought, so I rejected it and walked out, rationalizing my behavior. *I mean, I had a medical card; it was legal!* I was like a child, having a temper-tantrum with my arms crossed. Crazy!

I left there like wow, she knew what she was talking about because of how she called me out, but it's not the weed that's the problem. Talk about delusional. She was right about everything else.

I wish she had directly addressed the issues I faced in my marriage. In my mind, the weed helped me and my marriage. In reality, my problems were deeper than just weed, and smoking didn't help my situation. It opened the door to other spirits that were influencing the situation. True story.

My smoking had increased from a few times a week to a point where I couldn't get high enough. Something weird started to happen. I would finish a blunt and put it out and roll another. I had never done that before.

Uh, oh. My high wasn't lasting.

I spent a minimum of $40 daily to every other day getting the top shelf (better quality weed) at the dispensary for my daily habit. If I was smoking with others, I would spend more. I tried to hurry with my clients on the days I knew I had to re-up. I had to get to the dispensaries before they closed. If I missed getting my "fix," I would have a major attitude.

Eventually, I started to do what I said I would never do—smoke on Sundays, Tuesdays, and Thursdays because I went to church on those days. I wanted to set those days apart for God. However, I started to light up afterward.

I knew I was in over my head when I was up at 6 am on a Sunday, doing a wake-and-bake (smoking weed upon waking), having coffee, and then going to church. That thing had gotten out of control.

I realized that it controlled me at this point, but I didn't know how to stop. I needed help.

SUPERNATURAL INTERVENTION

On Friday, August 7th, 2015, I was on the porch, drinking with my husband and my cousin Monica. We were hanging out, laughing, drinking, and talking, as was customary for us. I rolled a blunt and was smoking. A blue minivan pulled up, and it was Wanda. I immediately put the blunt out and went into the house to the bathroom to wash my face, brush my teeth, spray, and all that to remove evidence.

I came out of the bathroom and went back outside. Wanda was talking with them. As I came out, Frank and Monica got up to go inside. Wanda and I sat on the porch, talking. She said not a word about anything directly. She knew I would drink, but she didn't know I smoked. Later, I would find out that she thought it was one of them who smoked because she smelled it outside.

As we sat there, the Holy Spirit within her started talking to me about my walk and what I presented to people. She said that what I do can affect their walk and that I shouldn't be a stumbling block to anyone.

See, my cousin Monica was coming to church, but she was not yet baptized. My husband and I attended regularly, but we were still engaged in our usual activities because we didn't have made up minds.

She went on to say that I had been called to a higher purpose, that there were certain things I could not do and places I could not go, and that my life was different now, and I had to walk in the newness of my life. She still didn't directly address it or call it out.

That was Friday. I listened, and I received that word. Saturday came, and I smoked and enjoyed my day as I would any other Saturday. I worked in the salon, and everything was normal.

On Sunday, August 9, 2015, I went to church and went up for altar call prayer and got Pastor Roy. He prayed over me and said that I had to walk in a way that was fitting to my call, that the Lord was calling me higher, that people watched me, and I could be a stumbling block if I wasn't careful.

He asked the Lord to strengthen me to walk worthy of the call on my life. He was saying similar words that I received from Wanda, and even more. I was shaking from the power I felt at that altar; this was amazing. I knew I was done!

"Thank you, Lord! It's clear to me!" I cried with outstretched arms at the altar. *Lord, you are so real!*

That was the last day I smoked. I threw away whatever I had left. I threw my weed grinder away and everything. I have not smoked since. And the best part is that, in December of that same year, my cousin Monica was baptized!

I'm thankful that I didn't cause her to stumble. It's been almost five years since the writing of this book, and that is the *longest* time I have ever gone without smoking.

SUPERNATURAL INTERVENTION

Glory to God!

I knew I was delivered for real because I had been around weed, and I didn't have any urge to smoke. I remember throwing my grinder, tails, weed, and all the paraphernalia away previous times and going right back to the trash and digging it out. I would say, "Who am I kidding?" But not this time—it was different. The Lord took the desire away! Hallelujah! I was not the same when I left church that day.

I asked the Lord why He allowed me to smoke for that long when He had the power to just take it away immediately. He didn't answer that specific question, but He said that *people are in His church just like I was, doing what I was doing. They were smoking, getting drunk, getting high on other substances, and coming to church as though all was well. They weren't confessing their faults one to another, seeking prayer, or repenting for their behavior; they were hiding, and it grieved Him.* I felt terrible—not only for my behavior but for that of my brothers and sisters—and I prayed for them.

Since then, I've had a burden for the Body of Christ. I pray for the Body often; I know the difficulties of life—even a saved life. It's easy to get lost in vices. We must control our desires rather than letting them control us.

We are all open, naked, and exposed to God. He sees all. It feels amazing, to be honest. It's freeing. God was saying to me that He needs us to go deeper in Him. Higher! He wants to take us to new heights, new levels in Him. We forfeit that by our decisions and life choices. We must not live to our flesh, but our spirit. We must renew our minds.

Truth is freedom!

THE WORST PAIN

I had just opened my very own storefront salon on May 31st, 2016, and God truly blessed me. I had more clients than at any of the salons I'd worked at previously, which amounted to more income. I was doing amazing, and things were moving swiftly for me.

Friday, June 24th, 2016, rolled around, and I was twisting dreadlocks for my client Mike; I also had two clients sitting in the lobby. My phone rang, and the news I heard would forever change my life.

It went like this:

My brother Len called me; I answered saying, "Hey Lil Bro," my customary greeting for him. "What's up," and I say this in my usual cheerful John. He says, "She gone, sis."

"What?" I ask, confused.

He says in a low sad voice, "Momma, not breathing."

I said, "What do you mean? What are you talking about?" I felt my heart beating faster like it would come out of my chest; and my voice got louder.

He continued, "She laid down for a nap and never woke up. She's gone, Sis. She's gone."

"No!" I screamed and dropped my phone, falling to my knees, still crying.

Mike grabbed me as I was falling to the floor. My other clients ran into my suite, and I watched everything happening as if I wasn't there like I left my body; I saw and heard myself wailing. I heard my voice trying to explain what was going on because they were asking.

I heard Mike tell someone to get Hicks from next door, and then Hicks was there trying to calm me down, and he started praying. He was attempting to give me hope that she wasn't gone. Yet something in me said she was, and I went numb. My clients, Judy and Monique, who were there, offered to drive me home or to my mom's or wherever I needed to go; they were truly kind to me, but I wanted to drive myself. It was a fight that I won. I watched myself drive, and them following closely behind as I drove the 10 minutes to my home and waited for my husband, who immediately came to get me.

My husband was talking, trying to reassure me. I heard his voice, but no words resonated with me; I was in a daze.

"How is my mom gone?" I thought...."I just saw her on Monday." She can't be gone. I didn't believe it.

Nothing compared to the pain of losing my mom. I never blamed God, but I did ask "why" more times than I can count. *Why did she have to go so suddenly? Why couldn't I have more time with her?* I thought she would live a long time because of how lively she was. She wasn't a sickly woman. Now and then, she would get sick. She took her vitamins and ate garlic cloves, and she swore by it. So, her death was just out of the blue and shocked the whole family and anyone who knew her.

She was a giver and loving, but she was also very outspoken and direct with zero filter. I have been embarrassed many times by the words that my mom has spoken. I say this with a smile. She was an original, that's for sure.

But she was strong, smart, an amazing writer, and highly intelligent. She had lots of insight into world affairs. How could she be gone? She had something to contribute to the world. Her mind had something to give.

We would talk a lot about history and current affairs. She knew her Bible front-to-back. She was just an awesome woman, and I loved her dearly. We didn't always see eye-to-eye, but that's normal.

I was teaching her how to maneuver on the internet and create a blog for her to share her writings. She had something to say. *She can't be gone.* I kept saying this repeatedly in my head. *There must be a mistake.*

Monday was our day. I thought as my husband was driving. *Mom, I was coming on Monday.* More tears fell.

She usually came to my home, and she helped me with laundry and cleaning and hung out with the kids; it was so awesome having her there. This is something she asked to do to spend time with us, and I, of course, compensated her because Mom wasn't working, and I wanted to.

She was incredibly fun, and it was great to talk with her anytime, not just Mondays. But Mondays, we were together in person. I would pick her up in the morning, and she stayed all day until a few hours after the kids got home for school.

So, the Monday before her death, I went by her home. She had said she wanted this week off to rest and stay home. So, I visited her. I stayed until my doctor's appointment. Just a routine Ob/GYN checkup.

I sat with her and laughed and talked with her. I shared pictures with her of the salon. She hadn't made it around to seeing it yet.

I told her if it works for her, I would pick her and Daddy up the following Monday. I happily explained how good God had been to me. She replied, "I see that." That was awesome. My mom said she saw the changes in me, and the decisions I made, that they were good ones. She actually let me talk about the Lord without shutting me down. That was a first.

Although she was inactive, she was a Jehovah's Witness, and that was still her belief. Usually, Mom would say something like, "What are you doing in that church?" and other things like that.

She certainly wouldn't listen to me talk about it. I wasn't upset with her. I understood. I was the same way with people at one point.

I shut them down or shut my ears down. The Jehovah's Witness religion was the truth, and all others were liars and of the devil. That was the belief. She got it. I got her.

But although she saw the positive changes in me and my life, she just couldn't let go of her religious beliefs.

But this day, she was so open to listen. She also became very deep. I remember as I was about to leave, we were standing up, and we hugged.

With both hands upon my shoulders, she intently looked me in my eyes and said, "I'm so proud of the woman you became."

"Aww, Momma, thank you, I appreciate that." Still standing close to me and looking me in my eyes, she continued, "You know I love Frank. I love the family y'all got together. You did good. You got it right this time."

I laughed. She was fond of saying that I finally got it right. Ha, ha! She said that often. She loved Frank so much. My dad loved him, too. That was a blessing. Anyway, she talked along those lines a lot and was serious with me.

"Tara, I love you. I want you to always know that." Mom was not even blinking! Or at least it seemed that way to me. That wasn't something I often heard from Mom. Especially a sober mom. No, it doesn't happen.

THE WORST PAIN

I said, "Momma, I love you, too," and then, laughing, I added, "You so deep today."

She smiled. "I just want you to know that I love you."

"I know you love me, Momma. I love you, too. Now, I have to go to my doctor's appointment before I'm late. Remember on Monday; I'm picking you and Daddy up to bring y'all to the salon."

"Okay, sounds good," she smiled, and we hugged. She said again, "Tara, I love you, and I'm proud of you."

I was laughing again as I walked away because my mom never did all this. It was nice, though. I left there on Cloud Nine. Even at thirty-nine, to hear my mom saying she was proud of me and loved me was everything!

Those words still replay in my head even today; I hold on to that precious last moment. I miss her daily. I love her dearly.

We pulled up at my parent's apartment, and there were tons of people outside their door. I saw them but didn't focus on them. They were a blur as I walked past. I just wanted my mom.

There were people in the living room of the apartment. I didn't speak to anyone; I went straight to her room, held her body, and laid my head on her face, and cried.

She looked so peaceful. Oh my, as I write this, it's painful for me. I can see her lying there on her left side, facing the TV.

THE WORST PAIN

My mom's body had started to get cold. Her room air conditioner was on, and I felt like that contributed. I laid on her, holding her, tears falling down my face, speaking softly to her.

She had her nightgown on and the remote in front of her.

Laying there as she often did, watching her shows.

According to the timeline my dad and brother gave me; it's believed that she passed around noon.

Nothing prepares you to lose your mom. I went through so many changes and depression. Her removal from my life was damaging to my psyche.

I felt like she was all I had in my mind and emotions— even though I was married with children. Even though I still had Daddy and my other family, I still felt a void. I didn't have her.

But my mom was all I had, someone *just for me*. I will try to explain the best I can. I was not the easiest kid, teenager, or adult. I had many emotional issues and angry outbursts but see; my mom *got* me. She understood and accepted me on a level that no one else did. *No one.*

I *got* her, as well. We were alike in many ways. Her loss left a void in me. She and I had a connection and a relationship like no other. I talked to her throughout my life about absolutely everything, and she gave me advice. Granted, I didn't always take it.

This is a loss that hit me hard. I think of my mom every single day. I remember her voice, her laugh, and the advice she'd given me. She was a phenomenal woman. I didn't stay off work or away from church long after my mom passed. I think I took a week and a half off, if that. I needed to stay busy. Quiet moments brought multiple thoughts that I didn't want, and so I kept busy.

You never think that when you leave someone, you won't see them again. That thought never entered my mind when I kissed her goodbye and told her that I would pick her up on Monday. Life is precious, and time is short. Time is the most important, and we can't get it back. I find myself looking at pictures and remembering moments with her. She was a precious gem to me.

Who else would have loved and accepted me like that? God does—and even more, I've come to realize. God saved me from depression and isolation during this time because I received what He was doing.

I didn't fight against Him. I needed Him to help me get through each day when I didn't want to leave my bed or eat. I needed His strength to smile when all I could muster up was tears. I needed to feel His presence because the silence was so loud. I felt alone and lonely. I couldn't help myself, and no one around me knew how to make me better.

God gave me a Word through Mother Johnson, the same wonderful woman who operated in the prophetic from the early morning prayer that I mentioned earlier. She called me the morning of my mother's funeral.

This was my Word: "Grief will come, but it will not overtake you; I am with you, and you are the lighthouse in your family."

He also confirmed this Word with another of His Saints to me. This Word was indeed true. I did mourn, yet it did not overtake me. I was not in bondage to grief. Praise God! Only He can do that.

From that day forward, I did mourn, yet grief did not overtake me. I still mourn, yet I have peace. The level of peace that God gives surpasses all human understanding. It's an inner peace that the world doesn't understand, nor can it take it away.

I found my peace in Jesus in the most painful place in my life. I'd never experienced that type of pain, nothing compared with me losing my mom. Nothing. Likewise, I'd never experienced that profound peace.

I still think of her every day. I still hear her telling me to do my laundry and clean my stove. *"Tarah,"* she would call my name, as though there were an "h" on end.

Thinking of her calling my name or even leaving me a voicemail makes me smile. I find myself becoming more and more like her—especially as it pertains to taking care of my home and family.

I used to say that I didn't want that type of life, but my mom worked hard for her family. We were well cared for, and I appreciate her now more than ever because staying home is tough work. It's a thankless job that never ends.

During recovery from a double mastectomy surgery and then later treatment, I became a housewife. This was never my plan, and I didn't like it at first. I kicked and screamed to the Lord with "Why?" and "For how long" and "When can I go back to the salon?" I couldn't get into it.

Mom loved taking care of us as a full-time housewife—even though she sometimes joked about threatening to run away—I'm not my mom. However, I realized I missed out on a lot when I was gone and working so much, and with the late hours that I kept. The dynamics of my family have changed since then.

These various trials had blessings all in it. My husband handled it as best as he could. I finally sat down and allowed him to be the man, father, and husband he needed to be for us all. I realized that through this that I never had before, there was a constant battle of wills between he and I. Personally, I didn't know he could take on the house bills and everything else, but with the Lord as his guide and strength, he did.

I had never sat back and let anyone take care of me. I had to have some control over everything. It was scary being dependent and vulnerable. But it shouldn't have been. Not with the type of husband that I have. He loves me and wants only the best for our family and me. But I did see it taking a toll on him after a while. I started praying, asking for a job. I had physical issues, and I could do something part-time. But the Lord said only to write. This was tough, especially when you're facing financial problems. My husband, although a believer, didn't understand that, but he went with it.

As I was at the close of writing this book, my daddy died from stage 4 liver cancer. *Lord.* I asked Him *how much can I take? This is too much.* He answered, saying that I was stronger than I thought I was.

My reply, a downcast, mumbled, "Great."

Follow me as I go over this timeline. On June 24, 2016, my mom died. On December 8, 2016, I was officially diagnosed with Stage 3 breast cancer.

In December, my dad was also diagnosed with Stage 4 liver cancer. It was discovered after a neck surgery that he had. He had been in chronic pain, and the surgeon discovered that cancer was spreading through his body—especially his spinal column. I had my first surgery on January 18, 2017.

My dad and I went through chemotherapy and radiation that summer. I watched him deteriorate; it was terrible.

My siblings and I were just watching this like it was happening to someone else. Why were we going through so much? It was tough. And Daddy told me how he missed Mom. If she was there, I genuinely believe he wouldn't have gone so quickly. But I don't know for sure—just a daughter's musings.

THE WORST PAIN

From May 2017 until October 2017, I watched my dad decrease in strength. He was physically changing before our eyes. I was still undergoing chemotherapy, and he was going into Radiation. When I started Radiation, he was on Chemo pills, and then his health rapidly declined. Chemo is no joke!

My strength was incredibly low, and so was his. I spent as much time as I could with him. My sister and I would take him to the doctor together and take turns. Jade was great with helping Daddy transition from the apartment he shared with Momma to moving in with her. I know it wasn't easy for her and my nephew Marcus, but they took good care of him.

Daddy told me that he wished he was young like me if he had to go through fighting cancer. He said he would have had more fight in him. He also wished my mom was there with him. He was in deep mourning for his wife that he'd loved since he was a teenager.

He was doing well until the chemo pills; after taking those pills, everything accelerated with my daddy. I remember in July of 2017, his Oncologist said that he would be on the chemo pills for the rest of his life, and there was nothing else that could be done for him. We left there with long faces and heavy hearts.

I watched a fun, vibrant, dancing machine waste into a shell of a man; by September, my dad was bones. His face had lost most of the fat, and he looked like a skeleton.

THE WORST PAIN

One day I sat over Jade's house to be with Daddy, and he had an accident (those were frequently coming). I washed him up, changed his clothes and linens, and I could tell how much he hated what was happening with him. You had to know my dad. This total dependency was not him.

He was sad. I am sad even writing this right now because I can vividly see it all. I could sense his embarrassment, and I said, "It's ok, Daddy. This is normal. I got you." And tears formed in his eyes as he said some things in a whisper. I didn't press him. I helped him back to bed, and I sat next to him and talked with him.

As time progressed, he started seeing spirits and ghosts all the time and talking to them. I remember he thought he had a cigarette in his hand. It was interesting and funny to watch. He lit the imaginary cigarette with an imaginary lighter and dumped it in an imaginary ashtray.

I remember Jade laughing and saying, "Daddy, there is no cigarette." But I told her to leave him be. Let him enjoy his "cigarette." We laughed and enjoyed that moment with him.

My brother Peter, Daddy's son from a woman he dated in Mississippi, and his family came to visit Daddy because they knew he only had a short time left. That meant a lot to Daddy. You could tell that he was happy to see them— especially his son.

I had some weird feelings during this time. My body was weary, and my cancer treatments were doing a number on me. I couldn't be there for Daddy as much as I wanted. I would come sit with him when I could.

When I did, we talked a lot. We were about to have an uncomfortable conversation that we'd never had my whole life. When I was in my twenties, I would say to him that he didn't treat me right, and he said that he loved me.

But at his bedside, when he only had weeks to live, I told him that I forgave him for everything and that I knew he genuinely loved and cared for me the best way he could. It was a special moment with tears rolling down my daddy's cheeks that I affectionately wiped away.

I wish I had said something sooner, but I'm also thankful for that time we had. I held on to him and laid my head on him, which I had never done in all my life.

JOURNAL ENTRIES

7/5/2017

Cancer sucks. Watching my dad get smaller and smaller and knowing that he won't get any better makes me feel very sad. I feel hopeless. I ask God for mercy for him. The oncologist says he has to take chemo pills for the rest of his life, and he will scan him every three months to see what the tumors are looking like. What will his quality of life be like after always having to take chemo? I hate cancer.

7/18/2017

I had a dream last night that my dad was going up to heaven. In the dream, it was like I was watching TV. I saw it happening and started praying and interceding.

9/2/2017

My dad is dying. I went to see him yesterday, and he is unrecognizable from the man he once was. He is all bones, and his eyes are sunken in. He has stopped eating, and he just wants to sleep all day. I hate to see him like that. He's in pain. His body aches constantly. I wish mom was here to be with him right now to be with all of us.

10/18/2017

I'm sitting here with my dad, watching him moan in pain. He can no longer talk, and he just grunts. His body keeps jerking. He doesn't seem to be aware of my presence. It's extremely hard to watch him go through this, and there is nothing I can do.

End of Journal entries

My dad died the next day after this last journal entry. We were all in the hospital room with him. I wept for this loss of this man, who had once brightened the room with his smile and had dance moves no one could match—even though they tried. My children were struggling with these losses, and I didn't know what long-term effect it will have on them. They both became more withdrawn after the death of their grandparents. Devin was terribly angry, and Tyler became silent. I was praying for my baby girls.

That year had so many highs and lows. It felt so surreal. Lord, this hurts. So much had happened, and I was amazed that I was strong enough to even get through it all. My dad's death brought back my mom's death, and it was extremely heavy. This time, I succumbed to emotions like disbelief and anger. I authentically needed the Lord. I was hurting on the inside so much, and no one understood. The outside looked fine, so people assumed I was fine. I wasn't. People would ask how I was, and I wanted to scream, "I am not okay!"

In such a brief time, I'd experienced a great loss. It was never-ending, the deaths. One call after another from family members and friends. I became numb. I would get offended because people didn't treat my dad's death like my mom's. I mean those around me. Do people have more sympathy for dead moms than dead dads? I don't know, but it felt that way. I was angry. It was all different. I didn't feel as if anyone understood my pain. I know I had to continue to live and take care of my household, but my husband didn't know how to comfort me during this time, and I felt further alone. He didn't always say the right things, and I would withdraw from him. I didn't think it was intentional, but sometimes people don't know what to say or do, and many do nothing. I stayed to myself.

This brought further clarity to me as I refocused not on all the deaths and the pain that I felt but on God's love and how He was still good. I looked at my family, and I would sit with God in my prayer room, sometimes in complete silence. It was comforting. But a new "me" emerged from all this pain. A "me" that was conscious of each breath, who was thankful and appreciated the gift of life. A "me" that was not going to sit down and conform to make you comfortable. A "me" that had a voice and would use it. A "me" that understood that although married, I am still an individual, a woman, and I had my own opinions that may not always agree with my husband. A "me" that understood we all must walk this walk before God. This new "me" is very aware and discerning. No longer am I going along to get along. I can say, "No." This new "me" values my time and my peace, unlike I have ever in my life. This "me" lives for God totally sold out without shrinking back. I love the new "me."

Hello, my name is Tara Tucker, and I'm a force to be reckoned with!

BREAST CANCER

Wednesday, December 14, 2016, Journal Entry

I must be very strong because a lot keeps happening in my life, yet God says He will never put more on me than I can handle. So, I have to be strong and handle it all.

I lost my mom and got cancer in the same year. But also, I got a salon and celebrated my first year as a homeowner. It's weird. Emotions. Joy and pain… anger and sadness. I am currently experiencing confusion and shock. I seem okay, outwardly, but inwardly, I am not. It's been six days since I received the news, and I am trying to dissect it all. Today, my dissecting consisted of a tall glass of wine, and then some. That isn't normal behavior for me and hasn't been in years, but I truly felt overwhelmed today.

I remember when I got the call. I was waiting on my next and last client. It was 3 PM on Thursday, December 8, 2016. Dr. McCarthy called and said that she had bad news. Somehow, in the back of my mind, I knew I had it. I knew it as I lay on the table, receiving an ultrasound and biopsy. I told her to go ahead with it after asking if it was okay to talk on the phone. Yes! I was not about to wait and come into the office—oh, no! So, she told me. Invasive ductal carcinoma. Wow. She reassured me that it was in the early stages and told me some info from my pathology report. She talked to me about a surgeon and other things. I was writing down what she was saying, but I was in a daze if that makes sense. I hung up the phone with her, and it was only then that I realized I was shaking. I said, well, okay, God. Here we go.

End of Journal Entry

I was sitting in the Webber Cancer Center, receiving Taxol, the chemotherapy that I was currently on while writing this chapter. It was the third chemotherapy medicine that I'd received. The first two were rough on my body. I was sick throughout the day on those. I went through that for two months before I was put on a less aggressive chemotherapy medicine for the following two months. The less aggressive one caused me lots of bone and joint pain, not sickness. But even then, as I was going through those rough times, God gave me some days of normalcy, for which I was grateful.

Still, I would often wonder how I ended up in a cancer ward, receiving chemotherapy. It's a shocker to hear you have cancer. I had just turned 40, and I had never had a mammogram before. My very first mammogram came back irregular. This is what happened. One day, when I was in the shower, towards the end of September 2016, out of the blue, I had a thought: *Do a breast exam.* So, I did. Raising my left arm, I went around my breast, slowly applying a little pressure. Everything felt normal. I raised my right arm and repeated the technique, only to pause. *This doesn't feel right,* I thought to myself. There was a lump on my right breast, near my armpit. It felt hard, and it was the size of a marble. I paused. *Lord, no. Please, no.* Somehow, I *knew* something was wrong.

I got out of the shower, not mentioning it to anyone and knowing that I needed my doctor to check, as well. I immediately scheduled an exam with my gynecologist. She saw me at once and confirmed that there was indeed a knot there that concerned her. She gave me a referral for a mammogram. I sat on that referral until after my birthday, which was coming up in November. I didn't want to think about it, nor did I mention my fears to anyone except Frank and

Monica. I kept it inside until I set the appointment up.

From the mammogram came an ultrasound and biopsy, which revealed that I had Invasive Ductal Carcinoma, which is a fancy term for Breast Cancer. They couldn't accurately stage it until surgery. She said it was a 2. After surgery, it was determined that I was a 3b, and I had 9 out of 12 infected lymph nodes that they removed from under my arm, resulting in a condition called Lymphedema, which made my right arm swell, and hand look like a mitten. Also, after tests, it was determined that I had BRCA2, which was a mutated cancer-c a u s i n g gene. It was suggested that my ovaries be removed within the next year or two because of the high probability of ovarian cancer. *Geeze. Leave my body alone!* That is what I wanted to scream.

Let me back up—I received the cancer diagnosis and didn't tell anyone at first. I received it while I was working in my salon. I was in shock, yet I continued and finished out my clients without mentioning a word. I laughed and talked as normal, but my mind was racing, replaying the conversation in my head. I cleaned the salon, and then I headed home. I drove home with no music or anything playing. I was silent, and I drove slowly. I knew that I had to talk to my husband. I walked into the house and put my purse and coat away. I went to the bathroom and said a prayer: *Help me, Lord*. I even cooked dinner before finally sitting down with my husband.

"Baby, the doctor called me." Frank had gone with me for my ultrasound and biopsy.

He stopped what he was doing and looking intently at me. He asked slowly, "What did she say?"

I replied, "That I have breast cancer."

I saw the tears well up in his eyes as he started to cry, and he just held me so tightly, and I burst out crying in his arms. All that time, I had been holding it in and dealing with it, but now, I could just release it in his arms. It felt like such a weight was lifted. "What are we going to do, baby?" I cried. He reassured me that God had me and had us as a family. We sat holding each other in silence for a time.

He and my cousin Monica went to my appointment with me. We met with the multidisciplinary team to meet the various doctors who would treat me and receive answers to our questions. One by one, we met and talked to the Cancer Surgeon, Radiologist, Oncologist, Social Worker, Nurse, and Plastic Surgeon. It was so much information, and I thank God for my cousin and husband being there with me. All I knew was that I had breast cancer, and I couldn't focus on anything else. Mechanically, I wrote down what they were saying because I do that. I can take dictation. My cousin and husband asked questions. I asked a few also. But it was just too much, overwhelming. I learned what to expect from surgery and the recommended treatment plan. I talked with the plastic surgeon about the reconstruction. You could tell that they did this regularly. It seemed too routine. This was my life they were speaking of!

Anyway, I found out I was Estrogen receptive positive (ER+), which meant the cancer attacking me would grow from estrogen. This was ludicrous to me, as a woman with estrogen, and they were telling me they had to suppress my estrogen with hormone therapy after I was done with surgery, chemo, and radiation. It was too much to bear. I wanted to run.

This was also during the holiday season, and I didn't want to ruin it for my children, so I didn't tell them anything. Another thing that was going on was my birthday dinner. It was a big deal turning 40, and I invited my closest friends and family to celebrate with me. I remember sitting at my birthday dinner that November, laughing and talking, wondering if I would live. These thoughts enter your mind facing cancer.

I had similar thoughts Christmas day watching my children open their gifts, wondering if I would be there the following Christmas day. The fear was real.

I had faith, but I can't lie and tell you I wasn't afraid. People with faith die too.

Eventually, I told people close to me and asked them to keep me in their prayers.

I told my children just days before my surgery.

It was difficult with my baby girl asking, "Mommy, are you going to die?" that was heartbreaking. I spoke to my children individually because of their age. They asked me questions but overall took it better than expected.

Talk about a reality check. I realized in the moment of facing cancer that my life was not in my hands. What could I do? Nothing mattered at that moment except my family and friends. I thought of God and them.

My prayer was, Lord, take this away from me. Give me the miraculous healing that I hear people have when they go back, and the tumor is removed. Angela prayed for me to have the miraculous healing, also.

It was such a tough time emotionally. My sisters in Christ prayed for me and gave me encouraging words. The Lord said that this would not be onto death, so I held on to that. I certainly wanted the testimony of having a tumor and getting prayer and deliverance from the bondage and spirit of infirmity, but it was not to be so. I had to go through the surgery and treatments.

As more people found out, they started contacting me and talking to me, giving me advice: "Take chemo," or "Don't take chemo," and, "Eat this way, eat that way." Many reassured me, saying, "Don't worry or fear. You know that God's got you." *Easy to say*, I thought. Yeah, I know, but I still worried and feared. *They* didn't have cancer. And *they* didn't know what was going on in my mind and body, so ultimately, I felt alone. I scoured the internet, looking for stories of ladies who were in my shoes. Finding them was like finding water in a desert. It was that deep for me. From the time of the cancer diagnosis and throughout the next year, I suffered from insomnia and could only sleep with medication.

On January 22, 2017, I heard the Holy Spirit say clearly, "This will be the year of reveals and revelations." I had just come home from the hospital. I didn't understand the Word, but I wrote it down. After that, my dream life was kicked up a notch during the times when I did sleep. I also followed His direction and started writing. My ears seemed to be unclogged or something because I was hearing Him unlike, I ever had before. My eyes were opened, and it was like I was seeing for the first time at 40 years old.

The first day when I received chemotherapy, I started becoming increasingly nauseous. Literally, after the nurse attached it to my port, and I sat for hours, receiving the poison that would kill the cancer cells in addition to my healthy cells, my body was weak, and I was truly *out of it*. Tuesday was even worse. So, I was extremely ill, and an evil spirit came to me on Tuesday, late at night, and said to me that I would die. He started tormenting me with those thoughts.

The voice I heard was aggressive, and his voice was messing with me. I said, "No, I will not. I will live and not die," and I told him to go away. The Word says to resist the devil, and he will flee. God gave me a Word that I held onto throughout my entire ordeal, and that was, "All will be well. This is just a process that you have to go through, and I am with you." He knew I was scared, and He encouraged me.

That demon did flee. But he came back at other times. He came to mess with my children or try to cause division in my home because I was weak physically, mentally, and sometimes spiritually. But thanks be to God. He is so good. He surrounds us with the people we need to intercede for us and keep us lifted and encouraged.

I received eight horrendous rounds of chemotherapy, followed by 28 rounds of radiation. I had my port put in before chemo and then removed after chemo. This was a physically, mentally, and emotionally painful and exhausting time of treatment.

Later that year, I started on Tamoxifen until after my ovaries and fallopian tubes were removed (which put me in menopause). Then I was put on Arimidex, which, per my Oncologist, I will take all my life. I'm praying that's not the case. Both of those treatments are for hormone therapy.

I then had my reconstruction surgery later that year. It was constant procedures from 2017-2018, countless surgeries. My body has suffered from the cancer treatment, and I now have new conditions that I battle daily. I am thankful, though. I am alive to tell it.

People tell me I'm brave to have fought cancer. It was extremely difficult. I hated it. My main goal was to keep focused on God and to take it day by day. Attitude is important when battling cancer, and I was mindful of mine. I loved my family and friends to check on me and spend time with me when I was physically and emotionally up to it. Support for my caretaker husband and me was necessary. People forgot about him and my children; they needed support also. I often prayed for them. Many times, I found myself cheering them up with all that was going on. Cancer affects everyone who loves you. It was a life-changer for my family.

I couldn't have made it without support. Now, I deal with the aftermath of battling stage 3 breast cancer. That's no walk in the park, and nothing is the same.

Everyone's cancer story is different, but we have in common the *knowledge* of what it's like to battle a disease that kills people every day. We know not only how it affects us physically but mentally, emotionally, and spiritually.

Many of my friends have lost their battle with cancer since completing my treatments, and I've dealt with survivors' guilt. Why them? Why am I still here? I cried many times, and then fear would set in, thinking I would die next. All of this has just been deep. Heck, the last four years of my life have been heavy.

But God has been faithful, and I will end this chapter with a scripture that I stand on Romans 8:18 KJV "For I reckon that the sufferings of this present time are not worthy to be compared with the glory which shall be revealed in us."

BREAST CANCER

EMBRACING CHANGE

I was staring in the mirror at a face I'd never seen before—a clean, bald head, no eyebrows, and barely any lashes. The chemotherapy had taken my hair, and I was clean all over my body. I slowly lower my eyes to my breast. These were not *my* breast but a foreign material inside of me. I start to cry as I reached out to touch them. They felt so far removed from me even while being attached to me.

I looked at my scars, marks from radiation, discoloring of my skin, and various scars from the different surgeries. I look at my right arm and hand. They were swollen. My hand looked like a mitten. I had excess fluid in my stomach.

Lord! Jeez, this is heavy! Help me be okay with this.

That was my new normal.

Going forward, I began to embrace my newness. I am alive! I still have an assignment here on Earth! Praise God! I promise to live, Lord, and exalt You for all the days of my life! Get the glory out of Your life!

I had a newfound passion for living that many around me didn't understand, and I could tell. In general, they got the idea of it, but did they understand that I was not the same? There was no "same" just "new."

I was such a busybody; now, I'm more relaxed or chill. Silence has become a friend of mine. My husband and children often ask me, "Are you okay?" and I smile and say, "Yes, I'm good," because I am. I'm alive. That may seem deep to them, but even if things are not okay, I am.

Each day is a gift. I sing and dance more than ever. Life's good. Not based on circumstances but because I'm here to take part in it! I'm here! Praise God!

God started renewing me and increasing me spiritually as I sat home reading, writing, and sitting in His presence. I had never spent this much time with Him before. I made a room in the basement, my prayer room. Initially, it was going to be my woman's cave decked out with an entertainment system and all the works, but I set it aside for God.

I thought of all these things as I went through my chemotherapy. I reflected on my life that was so crazy, filled with extreme highs and lows. When I experienced some calm, I thought that all was well, and I was done. I was learning by going through these trials, and there was more for me to tackle and accomplish.

Through this trial, the Lord showed me how to be a better wife and mother, not just based on how my husband or children were acting, but because of what He told me to do. Not an easy task at all. He showed me through His Word and other mature women of God how I ought to behave and conduct myself as someone who followed

Him and how to allow my husband to lead and be the head—even if I didn't feel like doing that. Besides, I've learned how to fight my battles and which ones to fight. Also, to just be quiet sometimes. I didn't always have to have the last word. (*I just dropped a major key if you have ears to hear*).

These were also things my mom would say to me. I didn't always listen.

My daughters suffered a lot during this time because they were grieving their grandparents and their mom. My children have not been the same since all this transpired. Heck, I wasn't the same. I'm *not* the same.

I keep changing, and I know how short life is. I survived something that kills people every day. I don't like people who are always complaining. I just feel like, *really*? *Well, it can be much worse.* I want to love people. I don't want to fight and argue. If I do, I want it to be over as soon as it started. I'll even apologize to keep the peace—even if I'm not wrong.

My parents are gone, and I'm here. Many of my friends are gone from the same disease I survived. I am new in many ways. I don't care about superficial things as I once did. I lean on the Lord for every single need that I have. Once you've experienced as much loss as I have, your outlook changes.

How can I be the same? As God keeps taking me from faith to

faith, I shed old ways of thinking and welcome new ones. Molting like an insect, shedding my old self as a new and improved one emerges. I will continue to shed, expand, and grow. It's a process. Through the process, the enemy is there, whispering and planting doubt and fear in me; yet I prevail because my understanding is that I am a winner, and he is a defeated foe. I am a conqueror—even more than he. So, I am fighting from the position of a conqueror. I enter the fight with that mindset.

I thought I loved myself in the past; I didn't. But I do now. Through the loss of my breasts, to the loss of my hair on my body and head, and even to my estrogen being low and not feeling very feminine, I learned to see myself the way that God sees me. I love me. I'm beautifully and wonderfully made.

This body has been used and abused for most of my life. I thought it was the best part of me and what I had to offer. But I had my eyes opened, and it showed me that I am worth much more. I was now with a man who didn't require my body as much as my mind and heart. He was someone who wanted me even after learning the truth about my past.

My priorities have shifted, and I am not allowing people to waste my time. Time is the most precious thing on Earth. You can't get it back once it's gone.

People get offended when you stand up for yourself. Have you noticed that? When you say, "No, today is about me." But I can't continue to let them waste my time. *A Sista has things to do!* That's where I am now. I must do it—even to my family. They understand. Mom needs time to herself to be good for them and for what the Lord needs her to do.

God and Family are foremost. Seek His Kingdom—everything else will work out.

This pain I've experienced in life, and this overwhelming loss, has propelled me further into going after my dreams. I believe in myself—even if no one else does. If God is for me, then it doesn't matter who's against me. The overwhelming joy and peace within me is indescribable, and no one can take it away from me. I can only give it away, and I choose not to do that. I believe in God, and I believe in me. He put gifts in me, and I am seeing myself through the correct lenses now. I have goals that I will accomplish. Pressure makes diamonds, and I'm sparkling, baby! I'm a jewel!

GOD'S WILL VS. MY WILL

I was able to not only come to grips with the disease that was attacking my body but also with my parent's deaths. Please note that this would have been impossible without God. Impossible with His peace that surpasses all understanding. Impossible without His covering.

During this time, God allowed me to see myself, and He stripped me and helped me refocus. I didn't realize how vain I was until my outer appearance was stripped away. I learned early how the external appearance was important and used it to my advantage. Later I knew how the inner parts were *more* important than the outer.

I trusted my money, and that dried up. I trusted in myself and my ability to be independent until I was placed in a dependency position. I realized much later in life that God was with me always, even when I was younger.

God showed me many times how we think we are putting Him first until He shows us that we are not. Believe it! It's a shocker—especially when you are active in the church.

It's easy to look at your circumstances and say, "Why me?" or blame God. I want you to consider another possibility. Consider trusting Him, as He knows the end from the beginning. When we see a little kid running in the street, we tend to grab them; sometimes, we yell, or they may get a spanking, but they will receive a stern talking-to because we know the dangers of what could happen. In their innocence, they do not. God deals with us the same way.

Many situations befall us, and we have no clue why. Some may not understand the concept of sin or our fallen nature. God created us and has a plan for each of our lives. His spirit is like a GPS, telling us the way to go, and when we go off the path, He reroutes us. Even the GPS is silent sometimes, but it reroutes us when we go off the course, as does our Heavenly Father. But to know the path, we must be tuned in to hear. Each day, the Lord is fine-tuning my hearing.

A lot of it comes with my desires. Do I *want* to hear? And if so, am I *positioning* myself to do so? Meaning, am I putting time aside for Him, reading His Word, listening to the preached Word, sitting in His presence, and praying? What actions am I taking? See, I realized this was not a one-sided relationship because, in the natural world, one-sided relationships don't last.

How do you move forward? First, you must exit. You leave one place to go to another. I couldn't stay in that place. To move forward, I had to exit. Close that door, that chapter, and move on, even if I didn't know what was next. It's a faith walk, and honestly, it can be scary not knowing the next move. I like to know everything. "What's happening next Lord," I would ask at times and was met with silence. If I could see all the moves, I didn't need faith.

Doubt would enter my mind coupled with fear of the unknown,

and that is not from God. Submit yourself to God, resist the devil, and he will flee. That is what the Word says. We can't resist him if we don't first submit to God. I submitted, and in doing that, I was able to resist him. Even now, I can see when he rears his ugly head. He comes to entice, harass, torment, and deceive, among other things.

Throughout all my experiences since meeting Jesus, I understand why we have trials and tribulations and why we must endure—especially when deliverance is delayed. My endurance has been strengthened. I'm stronger than I thought, and when I was weak, I would rejoice in the Lord because His joy was, and is still, my strength.

One of the biggest stumbling blocks on this walk for me was the insistence of my will versus God's will. I didn't realize that I was asserting my will over His at all, but I was. God will put us in a position where we must depend on Him. He allows us to be overwhelmed so that we can seek Him and see Him in all situations.

He wants us to know that He is more than able, and when things are going well for us consistently, we may think we did it. We tend to pray less and fast, even less, if at all. We say with our lips that we honor God, but our hearts can be far removed. It will show up in our actions.

I learned that I couldn't be everything to everyone. I learned to depend on God for absolutely everything. My morning starts with prayers such as, "Lord, let your will be done this day. Go before me and set my path straight. Let all things be done and said for your glory." And you know what? I have no idea how that will show up from day-to-day.

Jesus wanted me to take inventory of my life, so I did. I also had to look in my mirror and see the ugliness, the selfish ambition. I was doing what I wanted and totally independent. What God showed me is that my independence was from my husband and God. He let me see that I was still that little girl scared to open totally up for fear of someone taking advantage of me. You see, dependency is a very vulnerable place to be. Dependence allows people to hold things over your head and say what they do for you. That's a position I never wanted to be in.

I had to step out on faith and in complete submission to Him.

As I said, I had a flourishing salon, and my income was high, and I could see a bright future in the hair industry. In fact, I was planning to attend school to get my instructors' license in January 2017. I wanted to teach and be a platform hairstylist. Hair was on my mind all day. I thought of styles and marketing and looked at pictures and videos. I was constantly learning. I even dreamt of techniques that I would try. So, imagine my surprise when, after my double mastectomy, I didn't think of hair at all. I was confused. I had no desire for it. There were no more hair dreams. I chalked it up to my mind being clouded with the cancer situation and mourning my mom.

Shortly after, the Holy Spirit spoke to me in my private prayer time and said to close my salon. Okay, so now, I thought I needed my hearing checked. God could not be talking to me like that. That must have been the devil trying to trick me. God gave me the skill and opened that door for me to do hair, so why would He close it? Then, I had a dream that spoke to my spirit. In my dream, in February 2017, *I was back in the salon, healed and working. I had a client in my chair, and a lady walked in and said, "What are you doing here? You have to close the salon; you can't be here."* And then I woke suddenly.

After that, I reasoned with myself that He must mean for a few months after my treatments. When I felt better, I gave my landlord a date of return, but it was not to be.

The next time that I heard anything about not going back was through Mother Johnson. I went up for prayer, and she told me that God said that I had to stay close to Him and close my salon, as He was transitioning me to full-time ministry, and that He did bless me with the open doors to the salon but that I had put it above Him. That door was now closing. I had to sit down with God and let Him teach me through His Spirit. This was now the 3rd time I'd received a word to not go back to the salon and close it.

This was a hard word to receive. I understood it, but it's not what I wanted to do. Who was I apart from doing hair?

Besides, I didn't want to be in full-time ministry. I ministered to people in my chair. Wasn't that good enough? I prayed with them, if necessary. I wasn't looking for more than that. However, God had other plans for me. At this point, I had to relinquish the control that I thought I had and let Him have His way because His way was better.

He knew my path better than I did. And I realized that if I wanted His results, I had to do it His way. In obedience, I closed up shop and didn't look back, at least not right away.

My husband was even looking sideways at me, like, "Babe, are you sure about this?"

But I said, "This is what God wants me to do, and I'm going to be obedient."

He said okay, and he encouraged me from that point on. That was a far cry from the first time in our marriage when I was out of work. This time we were taking this faith walk together. Finances were different, of course, but we had what we needed.

Fast-forward to a year after my first chemotherapy, I was sitting on a stage at my book signing. *A book? Me?!* Okay, so, yeah, God has plans that we can't even imagine. Not only that, I founded a women's prayer group under the direction of the Lord called "Jewel's Ladies of Prayer." Also, after my book signing, I started a video broadcast based on my devotional, "Going Higher: 12 Weeks of Reflection for the Woman of God." My show is called "Going Higher Together."

I don't know how long I will do the show. God is leading me. I am following, sometimes feeling unqualified for the blessings. However, I am careful to think positive when it comes to this. He does things for me because HE IS GOOD, not because I am. In this walk,

I've learned that He can have me go in a different direction at any time. Staying in a position to hear Him and then follow with obedience is a must.

All I had to do was keep walking in my truth and speaking my testimony, and it helped people. I'm not a scholar. My writings have mistakes. I am just Tara, telling my story and experiences in an authentic way that hopefully people can relate to. My show also allowed others to share their testimony. I also started a blog entitled "Coffee and Scriptures," in which I post Words from the Lord, devotionals, and encouragement.

My life wasn't over; it was just rerouted. I didn't know it at the time. I was needed at home, and God knew that; I was chasing the dream and the money as I always did. However, through submitting in my home, I was learning to submit to God. I can't say I am submitted to God when I wasn't submitted to my husband.

The Lord got me to walk the walk so that I could be effective and talk the talk. He knew that I was heading into the ministry, and He started to prepare me from the moment that I was saved. However, it accelerated when I was fighting breast cancer, and in my obedience, He showed Himself to me more.

Walking in obedience requires great sacrifice. Many miss the deep things of God because they aren't willing to sacrifice their will for His. I thought I was doing that and found out in many cases that I was not. But a wonderful thing about my Heavenly Father is that He will align me and make my crooked path straight. What am I saying? I want to share a time when I believed that I was walking in God's will, but in fact, I was walking in Tara's will.

Remember back in January 2017 when I had my double mastectomy? Well, shortly after, the Lord said for me to write my testimony in a book, this book that you're reading. I was hesitant, of course, because I have done many things, much that is very embarrassing to my family to get out, but He said to be transparent, and He will handle the rest. Because it wasn't about me, it was about the souls that would be saved and set free from my testimony.

Okay. So, that is what I started to do—write my story. As you learned from reading earlier, the Lord gave me instructions to close my salon. I could have decided to go back and not to obey, but I chose to obey. In that obedience, we didn't have the same money that we were accustomed to having in the home, but God made sure that we were cared for. He gave us Divine Favor.

I was writing daily and many times in the wee hours of the night. I would then break, of course. I was first recovering from the surgery. It was tough on my body and everyone in my household. I couldn't raise my arms or wash myself up. I had drain tubes hanging out of my body. It was disgusting. But I would type, and that was therapy for me. I would start to write out my thoughts. This continued through chemotherapy. I was making major progress with my book. I hadn't gone back to church full time yet and was recovering and writing.

When I was working on an anthology called *Screams from the Church Pew*, the Lord downloaded another book to me called, *Going Higher*. He gave me the blueprint and everything. I put this book out in less than two months. I learned through these processes that God was showing me His vision for my life in part. There was so much that He was showing me, and I thought it meant that I had to do it now. I kept starting business ventures or whatnot because of the vision, but it wasn't time.

Obedience is what He is looking for.

He told me *this is only the beginning*.

It's in His timing. I started many projects and worked with others when He didn't tell me to do that. I thought because I saw some of the vision, it was ok to do. I learned the hard way that God will open and close doors. He orders our starts and stops. Although I tend to try to do everything at once, the vision is not for now.

He is still working on me.

I had to regroup, stop listening to people tell me what I should do, and only listen to what God says to do. This angers some that don't understand my movements, but I've learned to move differently as one sold out to the Lord. This wasn't always the case because I've been chastised a few times, but I learn through my experiences, and I confess my error, repent, and move on.

This book you are reading is my "book of promise," so to speak.

Why? Because this was the first book the Lord told me to write, and although I started it, I completed two others before going back to this one. I also created a business and a variety of other endeavors.

Birthing this memoir was no easy task. The labor pains were intense, but His will had to be done.

God's will for my life comes to me in dreams and in the small, still voice, which He confirms through my spirit, His word, His people, and my pastor. I have had over 100 dreams from the Lord thus far. He communicated with me through dreams, and more recently, with visions.

He has anointed me and blessed me in such a way that I am in awe. He has gifted me with spiritual gifts and shifted me to be around mature, spiritually powerful people. All Glory to God!

I have so much gratitude to God for changing my life. I didn't even believe that any of these gifts were available today. I thought they had died with the Apostles. Yet, here I am, seeing the Spirit move in my life and the lives around me with miracles, signs, and wonders. He is a wonder.

My past doesn't disqualify me—just the opposite. It equipped me with the knowledge that I could only gain with experience.

Nothing is wasted with God—remember that.

DEAR GOD

I wrote this while laid up, recovering from yet another surgery. I was in pain and emotional. 2016 and 2017 were two of the hardest years of my life. As I was writing, I would hear the Holy Spirit respond and record what He said.

December 5, 2017

Dear God,

I'm trying. I'm resting in you. Today I'm reflecting on it all. I know you've been with me. You've been by my side and in front of me. Lord, sometimes I want to scream. Sometimes I want to cry. I am so strong, and I hold things together, but I don't always want to. I have to. People are watching. My daughters are watching. My family, clients, and strangers. Church members...

I'm an example, right? That's what you told me. I'm an inspiration and have to show people how to walk this thing out. I'm all for that most days. Lord, I'm trying. Today I'm reflecting as I lay here in pain. Right now, I am fighting emotions. I am in my feelings. It's a rarity these days, as you know.

I'm down again with another surgery. Almost at the finish line, my cousin says. Yes, cousin, almost. But what's the finish line? Truly? I will always have to deal with something since the diagnosis. A year ago, today, I had tests done to determine if I had breast cancer. The results, of course, were positive. And thus, the journey began—a new Journey.

Don't get me wrong, Lord, I'm thankful to be alive. I'm thankful for growth. But my body seems like it has never recovered. I don't care what I look like on the outside. I don't feel the same. It's weird.

I'm a different me. A better me. Sure, spirituality I am. I wish I was courageous enough to go with no boobs. This surgery sucks. But I'm not sure I want that or just want to be left alone and speaking from that place. Right now, Lord, I'm overwhelmed with my limitations from surgery. I'm so active that sitting down is foreign. I feel unproductive.

Lord, you've allowed so much to happen to me. So much... I miss my mom. I wish I could talk to her... hug her... hear her say my name and laugh with me. My mom understood me best. I miss my dad. He was so fun—just a cool guy. I cry for them. Everything happened so fast, Lord. Just a year. Lord, help me!

Before I was saved, I didn't have all these problems. Now, I've lost my mom and dad, and I am fighting a disease that kills people every day. Yes, I'm in remission, but my doctor says my reoccurrence rate is high, so she will be watching me for five years. That is on my mind. I have to have another surgery next month. That is on my mind.

All will be well! You are my Healer. Yes, Lord. I know. I thank you.

I'm anxious, I believe, for it to be over. What a long year it's been, Lord. Not to you, though. A day is as 1,000 years for you.

This journey is so rough emotionally, and no one around me understands.

Lord, I'm trying. I lay here trying to be comfortable when all I can do is stay on my back propped up on pillows. I can't raise my arms. Yes, I know it's temporary. I try to stay focused on that fact.

I am thankful that my daughter is driving herself to work and school. What a blessing! I hate that I have to rely so much on her to clean and cook when she's home. She is the sweetest and does so much for her mommy. My youngest daughter pouts, when asked. Teenagers, SMH, LOL! But she does it. Sometimes, joyfully. Sometimes, begrudgingly... she's a sweetheart, too, but she has a lot of my sass, that's for sure. But honestly, why do I have to ask anyway? They know that I keep my house clean. Just do it! Because I can't. I take good care of them all!

Lord, I'm trying! You say not to worry and just rest. So, what if there's a little clutter? So, what if there's a few dishes.

No worries. Heal daughter.

You say to be thankful, and I am. I'm thankful that I have a husband who loves me and works hard to take care of us. I am thankful for my beautiful children.

You know what? I feel guilty sometimes that I can't do the regular things around the house. I feel guilty that I'm not ironing my husband's uniforms. I know I can't right now. I know I'm limited. It's temporary. Yes, God. I know.

Is it impatience? Forgive me, Lord. But I wish I could. Lord, it's so hard to ask for these things. My momma did that to me. There is still pride in me, Lord. Continue to purge me. I feel guilty for resting for doing anything for myself. I'm tired of being poked and prodded and tired of surgeries.

Sometimes, it's lonely, this route You're taking me on... these wonders You're showing me. Who would believe me? People believe what they see, but You've shown me to believe what I don't see.

You've shown me how to see in the Spirit. I can't articulate your greatness. Lord, I'm trying. You've told me to rest and not worry. And You know that I do that. Forgive me today. I'm venting. I haven't slept well—my body aches. I hate complaining. I feel weak when I complain.

This is all a part of my process. I'm on a journey. You've taken me to a higher level, and You aren't done. I'm grateful. I like to speak openly and honestly, Lord. My concern is always that I'm not bringing reproach to Your name. I don't want to do that—only glory.

I think of you all the time. All the time. Above anything or anyone.

You call me faithful? Well, Lord, after all, I've been through, all I've seen, all you've brought me out of, how can I not be faithful?

Lord, I'm trying! This thing is an everyday faith walk. No joke. No lie. And I can't make it looking at anyone else: Not my husband, children, friends, family, or church members. People let me down. I've let them down. But you... you are constant. You don't change.

Lord, I thank you!!! I give you glory and honor and praise because you alone are good! Thank you for capturing each one of my tears.

Thank you for changing my life!

I know that you've allowed me to go through so much as to be a testimony of your goodness—a testament to your ability to keep one in perfect peace. Today is a rare moment. I've had them sprinkled throughout this year. My joy overshadows any sadness I may temporarily experience.

It's so different in my household Lord. You've made me a housewife. I laugh. Who wanted that? Not me. I'm a career woman. Right? Ha! Lord, I'm trying! You've shown me that you are my Jehovah Jireh! My provider. The way my income is set up, it could be no one or nothing but you, Lord!

Why are my thoughts so different? Now I'm thinking of my family. I'm putting my husband first. My children... I used to put the salon first. Put getting money first. I used to be selfish, Lord. I can admit it now. I've looked at the woman in the mirror.

What have You done to me? You've made me soft! I don't even argue anymore. The fighter doesn't even argue or fight! Glory! I give a soft answer. Only You, God! I want to cook and clean for them. I want to spend time with them. I used to spend so much time at the salon. It was my getaway. Lord, You've made me a wife. A happy wife! And in response, my husband has become more affectionate and loving towards me. There is nothing he wouldn't do for me. Even cleaning, if I asked, LOL! But I get it. The man works very hard outside our home.

I know I'm loved. I feel it. I don't question my husband's love for me— even when he's overwhelmed. This has been hard for him, as well. I pray for him. I keep him before You. Strengthen him, Lord!

Lord, You are something else. Now, I'm smiling. I love You. I love the new mind that You've given me. I love my forgiving heart.

You've allowed so much to fall on me because I can handle it. I'm pretty strong, but where I'm weak, you show your strength. Lord, I thank you. I'm leaning on you and not my own understanding. My understanding leads to confusion. You aren't the author of confusion, nor do you operate in it.

Glory! I know when I'm operating in my flesh. Thank you for your discernment. I console myself knowing that you will perfect that which concerns me. I know that you will keep me in perfect peace when my eyes stay upon you.

I've become peculiar. I've always been different, but now I'm "peculiar," as one of your chosen. I find comfort in your validation. I find comfort in knowing who I am. I said life was easier before being saved. Not entirely true. It was me doing what I wanted on my own terms, not knowing who I was. It was me struggling to find identity through men, women, and also career. It was me smoking my day away, thinking I'm living it up because I could afford the good stuff.

Thinking because I was making the devil's money that I was good. I didn't have to ask anyone for anything. I was truly living in deception. That's what I know now. Lord, I thank you! The biggest thing you've done for me is to change my outlook. I can see! Not only with how I see myself but how I see everything else. I'm walking in complete transparency, and for a girl who lived most of her life lying and hiding, that's huge!

I have these moments of reflection. I may even experience frustration and sadness. I'm thankful that they are fleeting moments. I am so aware that it makes me not fit in anywhere. I can't say things because You've told me not to. I'm obedient above all. I fear You. I fear You more than I fear perception.

Lord, I go to church, and You've opened my eyes even there so that I see. Sometimes, I don't want to see. I feel sadness. You show me so that I can pray. I want everyone to want You and pursue You. You're so good! I see the complacency. I see the "It don't take all that" looks and energy. I see the real and fake love—even towards me. I can't act on it, except to show love and to pray.

You told me that some look at me in wonder. You told me that they are curious. Some are downright irritated. Show love. Yes, God. I will. I love that You are there because You are there. Your presence fills the place. Thank You for my church home. I spread my arms to You in submission. I don't care who's looking. If they knew what I did, then they would praise You, too! You are amazing.

Sometimes, I feel so much that it's hard to contain. Lord, I love You. Yes, I will rest. You know I'm thinking of my book and my deadline. I know You're laughing. You're laughing because You got me. You know all things. You gave me the book, so I know all will be well.

You know I'm excited and nervous about it. I want women to read it and be encouraged. There's no turning back for me. It's an elevator with no floors. I'll just keep rising but to Your Glory and not mine. You know how I feel about that. Your Will. Your Way.

Thank you for making me new. I feel strong and bold, knowing that if you're for me, who can be against me? You said, just "live it." My fruits will be seen from my household and then outwards. I see it, Lord. And others see it. This is a testament to your goodness.

You've come in like a whirlwind. I thank you. Everything's falling in line. It fell apart just to come together. Better than before. Stronger than before. Rest you tell me. Abide in you. Be encouraged. I hear you, Father.

The enemy tries me. But I'm aware. I'm not afraid of him. I see how he creeps in at my weak moments. I see how he messes with my children and husband. No weapon formed against me shall ever prosper. I don't care what it is.

I may be in bed and sore, but I can talk! My words have power! God, I thank You!

You've given me spiritual sisters. A bond that I've never experienced before. My sisters have been here, taking care of me. It brings me to tears, the love they've shown me. You've blessed me with a spiritual mother who loves me truly, who prays for me and gives me advice and correction, who spends time with me; she is a mother of many, and I'm thankful to be a part of her life.

Lord, I thank You. I will rest. I will abide. I will listen. I will obey. I will wait. I will acknowledge You in all my ways. I am grateful. You've orchestrated stops in my life that I didn't understand. Lord, I thank You.

I remembered the dream a few years ago; when I asked for a medium Slurpee, and You gave me one so large, I couldn't even carry it, LOL! You said that eyes have not seen, nor ears heard, nor has it entered into my heart the things that You've prepared for me because You know the thoughts that You think towards me.

God, I thank You! For every trial and every encounter! I thank You for my struggles. I thank You for my wilderness. Sometimes, You make me stay hidden. You allow me moments to come out.

Lord, I thank You. I walk in a grace that I didn't before. Continue to strengthen me. Continue to stretch me. Continue to mold me. Keep me on the Potter's wheel. There is no real happiness apart from You. You offer true contentment, True joy and peace. You make me randomly smile. Lord, I love You. I thank You. Keep me forever at Your feet.

In Jesus's name, amen.

DEAR GOD

THE COST OF "YES"

I had no clue what saying yes to God truly entailed and what it would mean for my life. Since I heard God call me out of my religion and my subsequent encounter in my bedroom in 2010, my life has been continually changing. God broke me but gracefully and lovingly. He broke me so that He could put me back together and make me fit for His use.

No *everybody kneeling ain't praying.* Many people live double lives, with hearts damaged by the hardships of life and people's hurt. Some have no clue how to trust God truly, so they appear to trust Him, put on a brave consecrated face for the world, yet they aren't living up to the standards they present. Many are hiding what they are going through, suffering in silence, for fear of judgment. But God is our judge. Those people we hide from have their situations. All of us are experiencing life together. No one is immune from the tribulations of life.

I was always searching for happiness or some form of it and wanting to live life on my terms, yet I've come to realize that it doesn't work. God created me; I didn't make myself. God knew and knows what's best for me as a good Father. Just like I know my children.

But as parents, we sometimes watch from a distance and let them live. They don't always make the best choices, but they must often ride it out and learn in the process. We help them out when they need it and sometimes let them fall because they need that too. Ultimately, we trust God with our children. At least, I do.

Everything I've experienced has made me who I am today. I had been searching for happiness in the world, but it was not until Jesus made Himself known to me that I found something better than happiness, joy. At the time, I wasn't looking for Him. He called me out of the world and manifested Himself to me in a real way. I didn't even know I needed Him; I just knew something was missing. There was a desire in me that only God could fill, pain that only He could heal, anger that only He could turn into joy. He did that and continues to take me a little higher with each life experience.

It didn't matter what I did in the past or the present. God didn't disqualify me from salvation because of prostitution or drug and alcohol use. My hunger for perversion didn't stop Him from calling on me. What mattered was whether I would relinquish the control I had over my life and yield to His will, and trust Him with my life. He loved me then, and He loves me now. The difference is, I *now* know that He does, and I know who He is and who I am. That gives me peace and makes me want to please Him.

I thought I was already walking in freedom by living life my way, on my terms, but it was bondage. God gives us perimeters for protection; however, the devil says, *do as thou wilt*. But the wages of sin is death. I thank God for putting me on the right track.

I am now okay with every part of me, not just the good parts. I'm ok with who I was because it helps me appreciate who I am now. I look in the mirror, and I accept the woman staring back at me. I know now that the feeling of rejection from my dad and siblings caused me to latch onto people for the wrong reasons; I've always craved love and loyalty. Feeling any rejection caused me to spiral out of control. I was also defensive and protective over my feelings and space.

I didn't trust men at all, but God showed me that I could trust Him and my husband. He taught me to love unconditionally through my marriage and my children. I didn't realize that sometimes in my independence, I treated my husband like I didn't need him until I had to sit down with my health challenges. Being dependent was scary to me.

My struggles strengthened me, showing me my capabilities. I've learned to endure. I still encounter trials, some extremely heavy, but I lean on the Lord and lay them at His feet. Also, the molestations released spirits upon me;

- spirits of confusion, which prevented me from seeing truth.

- spirits of perversion, which made me see through a distorted lens;

- spirits of rejection, which made me look for acceptance from anyone who would give it to me.

That perversion, rejection, and confusion made me live in a way that I thought was okay. As many others with similar testimonies believe, the way they live is ok.

Perversion called out to me, and I eagerly answered. Things I said I would never do; I did. As an adult, those sexual encounters I engaged in opened the door for dark spiritual activity to come into my life and influence my behavior. Not to mention the constant weed and alcohol that was a way of life for me; they helped me cope by "escaping." I learned that we are here in this natural world, but there is another world, a spiritual one that is more real than this one. A new revelation hit me. Once that happened, I could not act like I didn't know. I had to do better because I knew better.

Also, I learned in therapy that psychological trauma is worse than any physical trauma; it just stays there. Outward scars heal—Inner scars linger. My compassion for others has no bounds. I can't look and judge someone when I've done the things I've done. I don't know their story, but we all have one. I know God loves us, even the worst of us. I know nothing is too hard for Him or too big of an issue that He can't handle. Neither homosexuality, drugs, pornography, or whatever you may find yourself wrestling with.

God is bigger!

My "yes" has my God answering my prayers. Even still, that "yes" has taken me on a whirlwind from faith to faith, and I am still going.

God knew everything that I would face. He knew all that I did and loved me anyway. He accepted me and saved me. Me! I'm amazed. If He can do that for me, then He can do it for you. Do not count yourself out. Yes, tough times come, but I'd rather have a hard time with God than an easy time without Him.

Even after my "yes," I struggled with walking free versus being doubleminded. It takes time to walk out the process of sanctification with God. God is merciful, and He helped me to endure. He showed me how to trust Him one life moment at a time. And it boils down to trust and belief. People are quick to point out what you're doing or did, but what if you don't trust God yet? You're not letting your guard down and opening your heart for anyone you don't trust. You must learn who He is, just as with any relationship, and He will show Himself to you if you allow Him.

I won't force you to believe. How can I? We all have free will. What I can do is share what He has done for me. I was a degenerate, plain and simple—a nice one, but one, nonetheless. Imagine this: I was open and transparent in this book. Think about what I didn't say. There is more to my story. God knows everything and still loves me. God is powerful, and all He needs is your "yes." He needs a willing heart. Don't let your outward life keep you from salvation. Don't even let a broken heart or offense keep you from God. The devil is a liar. God loves you.

I have learned patience for others in my walk with God. He has forgiven me and I forgive others. I have no right not to forgive when all that He has done and continues to do for me. Besides, life is short, and the next is not promised, let alone a whole day.

Sometimes we don't understand what God is doing, but it's a walk of faith. I look at my children, and I don't understand some of the seasons they are in and the choices they make, but it's their season and their preferences. At one point, I cried daily with all that my youngest daughter was going through, and three times the Lord said, "Perfect love cast out fear." He gave me dreams and words. One word was, "You are crying because you don't know the outcome, but I know the outcome." That word right there got me all the way together! Not just with my daughter but in life. I have learned to relinquish the outcome, and I encourage you to do the same. Now I rest in His promises.

The Lord allows us to go through hardship to show us who He is and who we are. My children and my husband must develop and maintain their walk and learn God for themselves. We will all have to account for our own lives. However, I will continue to love and cover them in prayer. We all need to be faced with the mirror and then start the mind's renewal process. It is not an overnight process. Growth and maturation come from being close to the Lord. A relationship is necessary, and you can build it by praying, listening, waiting, reading His Word, and allowing Him to heal you from the inside out.

These heavy battles aren't always easy to carry. When it's too much, I call reinforcements; my spiritually mature sisters to pray and fast with me. God didn't intend for us to walk this Christian walk alone; this is not a solo mission.

My story continues to be written, as daily, I tell the Lord, "Go before me this day and set my path the way You want it to go." I am constantly saying, "Yes, send me. I will go," and in doing so, the Lord allows trials and tests as He "makes" me. It's not easy going through publicly, and often I feel on display. But I don't love my life unto death. I die daily and live for Jesus. If He needs me to speak my truth to help someone else, then that's what I will do for His Glory.

My life has been an interesting ride, and yet it continues. There were times when I questioned my mere existence. *Why am I here? Do I need to be here? What is my purpose?* I felt alone so many times. I realized that all those years without God, I was dead. I am now alive. I was dead in my trespasses and raising my children the same way. I tell them that having a relationship with God is most important. My husband and I were recently having a discussion where I said," Babe, if we don't do anything else, we must make sure we give the children God. They must know who He is." He agreed.

There is no real life without God, our Heavenly Father, and the Creator of everything. He loved the world so much that He sent His son Jesus here to Earth to die for our sins. He was raised from death to life. And for those who believe in Him, we are raised from death from our sinful nature to life in Him, spiritually speaking. Our old selves die, and He raised us to a new life in Christ. It's amazing, really. The Bible is not just a book, but its inspired text and the words are alive. I've learned in my journey that nothing is more important than God and my family; everything else is a bonus.

THE COST OF "YES"

If you don't have Jesus, you don't have anything. You just exist right now. He is real! That is what boggles my mind still today, as I write. He is real! He's more real than this chair I'm sitting in. He is not a figment of imagination; He is not the universe; He is the *Creator* of the Universe. You should pray and give thanks to Him. Jesus is the Creator of all. Whether you call Him Yeshua or Jesus; He is the great I AM. Jesus is in all and above all.

Today I look over my family, and I swell with emotion. I know what we have been through and what we are currently experiencing. Even still, I marvel at the way God works. Through my trials and broken places that I couldn't see my way out of, He mended everything. He made it beautiful in His timing. Perfect? Of course not, but *His presence* makes it peaceful, not the absence of problems.

I grow more in love with my husband every day. I see love when he looks at me and feels it when he touches me. I've learned to stay the course and fight for my family. There is a real enemy, spiritually speaking, that wants nothing more than to destroy families. Family is the foundation. We must fight the enemy and not each other.

God has changed me from the inside out. I thank Him and bless His name. If you allow Him to come into your life, He can change you for the better. If He's already in your life, continue to go higher in Him.

He forgave me for my past, yet I had to forgive myself. I had to let go and let God. I had to allow Him to remove the veil from my eyes. Once that happened, the reality of His love and forgiveness empowered me.

2 Corinthians 3:18 NLT says, *"So all of us who have had that veil removed can see and reflect the glory of the Lord. And the Lord--who is the Spirit--makes us more and more like him as we are changed into his glorious image."*

I thank God for His Mercy. God will meet you where you are and help you go where He has established for you. The Lord says that He knows the plans that He has for us.

My journey is unique to me, yet we all have one. I am not yet what I will become. I know God has great work in store for me. I see the vision, and it's big and scary. I know that I cannot achieve the vision I see without Him. Yet He promises never to leave or forsake me. He assures me that He is with me and to go forth walking in faith, not fear. You rest in that same assurance. He is with you.

And so, I have this newfound peace and rest that in all my years, I'd never experienced. In loving myself and finding out that I have a powerful voice, I've learned to love and be loved authentically. Also, to accept myself. I am beautiful, like me, and no one else. No comparisons. I am the righteousness of Christ, a daughter of the Most-High God. I've been called and chosen. I am proud to be a part of His Glorious Kingdom, and I will do my part to expand the kingdom, being the change, I wish to see.

~~

If you want to know the Lord and don't have a relationship with Him, I encourage you to seek Him in prayer. Ask Jesus to come into your life. Ask Him to forgive you for all that you've done. Don't allow friends, family, or even societal norms to keep you from a relationship with Jesus. Let Him know that you want Him to come into your heart and make Himself known to you. Authentically approach Him. Jesus met me in my bedroom, and I was deep in sin. Nothing you have done will keep Him from loving you. Repent and move forward in God. Repentance is necessary. Get a bible if you don't have one. I encourage you to read the word of God. That is how you will get to know Him. Shut out the noise. We are inundated with noise from tv to social media. Set some time aside and talk with your Creator.

I love you, and I pray that my story has blessed you.

ACKNOWLEDGMENTS

First, I thank my Heavenly Father, who saved my life, who loves me with an everlasting love, and who has gifted and equipped me to be so much more than I thought was possible. There is more to come, and I am excited about my future.

I thank my husband for his love and support. I never knew love until you. We've had an interesting ride, Frankie! Your love is true. You helped me to see that I was more than what I did. You saw beauty, where I saw ashes. I thank God for you. You see my blind spots, and I am enjoying this journey with you as we grow and mature in love together.

I thank my children, Tyler, Devin, and Deonta' who are full of love and laughter and bring me much joy. I love you three more than words could say.

I thank my cousin Monica for being there for me and believing that I could do this.

I thank my sister and brother for understanding that I had to tell my story.

To Momma Platt. I love you very much. God put you in my life

Acknowledgements

because He knew what was to come. He knew that I would need you. The advice, prophetic mentoring, and authenticity you bring into my life is unparalleled. I am blessed to know you.

Rest in Peace to my amazing friends and family that have gone on to be with the Lord. Love and miss you.

I am thankful to the Jewels: Your friendship and sisterhood is priceless. We are forever connected in sisterly love through Christ. Let's go global!

I thank my clients that were so supportive through everything. Some of you have become good friends.

I thank Prophetess Veontae Mann. The Lord divinely connected us, and you have become a mentor to me. You've pulled things out of me that I didn't know was there. You showed me other gifts the Lord gave me and helped me gain the confidence to walk in them. Thank you for being my spiritual doula at a time I needed you. I appreciate you.

Special thanks to Kim Gunn, Hanifah Burch, Rita Fields, Narkieta Williams, Author Dawn Brazil, and Gia Chandler; I appreciate all your help and honesty with my book. Love you, ladies.

Last but certainly not least, I thank my LAM Church family for being amazing! LAM is good ground! I love you all and appreciate you.

Thank you to all who support me. Blessings to you.

270

ABOUT THE AUTHOR

Tara Tucker is a Visionary, Coach, and Author of the books *Going Higher, 12 weeks of reflection for the Woman of God, You are Not Disqualified* and the anthology, *Screams From The Church Pew-Her Story, Gods Glory*. She enjoys blogging and mentoring in her nonprofit, Jewels LOP Outreach, of which she's the Founder. Tara owns Tucker Publishing House, LLC, a home for women to share their stories of inspiration and overcoming because she believes our authentic voices must be shared, making a powerful world impact. She is best known for her transparency and authenticity.

Her motto is "Live, Love, and Be Authentic." Tara hosts a LIVE podcast show every Wednesday called Going Higher Together. She was on many podcasts and shows such as Nikki Rich and iHeartRadio. Her heart is for women of faith to own and write their stories with clarity and confidence. She started the Black *Women Write* community to increase awareness and power of the Black Woman's' voice and gain freedom from writing.

Tara is a Transparency Coach and created Past2Purpose Academy to help other women like herself see that there is purpose beyond the pain. She lives in Michigan with her husband, three children, two cats, and one dog.

About The Author

Thank you for purchasing my Memoir, please consider leaving me an honest Amazon review.

Tara Tucker

About The Author